Foundations of Windows Server 2.0
Table of Contents
Page I of III

D1403859

Foundations of Windows Server 2.0
Table of Contents
Page II of III

Introduction to the book.

Introduction to the book:

There are a number of concepts in the field of server technology. In most developed countries, server technology exists in almost every part of our existence. Our cars have systems which interact with cell towers. Our homes have cameras which can be activated by smart phones. We order tickets for events via a website and doctors participate in group surgery between countries via streaming video. Our civilization has truly progressed to a technology-driven society. Due to the 1960's premonitions of what the future would include, I often hear people say, "Where is my flying car?!" When I hear that sentence, I smile to myself for I know the answer to that question. It is not that the flying car has not been created,..most people simply can't afford one so companies don't mass produce it.

The People Who need this book:

This book is structured in a format to allow motivated individuals to perform a number of high-order server technology tasks. Everyone whom purchases this book may not be interested in certification but simply desire to increase their knowledge in server technology. The subjects covered in this text are related to installation and maintenance of specific server technology such as Webservers, Domain Controllers and Server User accounts. The topics listed in this book are the foundation of Windows Servers. Thru the use of practical (Or what is referred to as "Hands-On") activities, the readers of this book will master the foundations of server technology and be able to perform all required tasks to implement the technology relying only on their accumulated knowledge developed through study, repetition and successful practice.

Introduction to the Field of Server Technology.

Introduction to the Field of Server Technology:

For those whom purchased this book to increase their knowledge in order to attain a certification in server technology, congratulations! You have the correct book in hand! The tasks which are displayed in the text are directly related to a number of certifications offered by Microsoft and Comptia. One of the excellent aspects of understanding one vendor of server technology is the ability to "Cross-Learn" other vendor technologies. The term "IP address" is used for servers, routers, printers and cell phones. These identities are used on all of the technologies mentioned above. The only difference is "where" you would insert the settings on each platform. This book is created in a "survey-course" fashion and was developed to give the reader the ability to firmly understand network technologies and to implement them in a production environment ("Real World"). The implementation is based upon "foundation understanding" and utilization of actual technology. Persons presently working full-time in the network technology field will benefit from the tasks in this text to learn the technology in order to enhance their organization's ability and functions. Persons who desire to enter the field of network technology will benefit from developing a practical understanding of what is required for servers to communicate and offer support services on a network or the internet.

Importance of having Network Certifications.

Importance of having Network Certifications:

There are a number of certifications available in the field of network technology. It is important that persons interested in the field understand the foundation of what each certification indicates in order to better position themselves in the job market. Many persons outside of the field have heard of different certifications. Certifications themselves do not make a person better at completing job tasks then someone who has no certifications. Certifications do have some essential truths to them which make their attainment highly desirable. It is regarded as true that a person who has certifications will possess the following qualities:

- **Greater knowledge of a specific technology than those without the Certification.**
  - Persons working in the field for many years primarily know tasks and technologies which they have been exposed to via job assignment or troubleshooting situations. The unfortunate association with the learning process is that the person has not been exposed to all of the primary features of a technology. Many features can save an organization money as opposed to purchasing many other devices which provide a function that the "on-site" technology already has built into it.

- **Display of letters for hiring entity (i.e., Human Resources, Selection Committee, etc.).**
  - Often times, the group responsible for the hiring process will not understand all the particulars surrounding the qualifications necessary to fill a technology position. In addition, after learning of all the requirements, it often becomes expensive to advertise all the desired criteria for an application to be successful in interview selection (Often times, job advertising companies charge the company looking for applicants based upon how many words are in the advertisement for example, $1 per word, charged every week the advertisement is available in newspaper or internet format). To compensate for the "word length" of the job advertisement and the review of applications eligible for interview, hiring entities often ask their associates for a better way of advertising a position with the least amount of "words" as possible. This normally results in the hiring entity being told some technology "abbreviations" to use instead of descriptive paragraphs.

Take the following scenario for example if the job announcement would cost $1 per month per word:

> **Option A: Human Resources person creates job announcement (Total cost about $51 dollars per month):**
>   ❖ The technology department needs a person who can perform the following:
>   1. Install Network Operating Systems.
>   2. Install, configure and troubleshoot Hubs.
>   3. Install, configure and troubleshoot Switches.
>   4. Troubleshoot network connections on computers.
>   5. Address printer problems.
>   6. Answer phones on the Help Desk.
>   7. Connect and install Category 5 cable in building.
>   8. Connect servers on LAN.

> **Option B: Human Resources person creates job announcement (Total cost about $8 dollars per month):**
>   ❖ The technology department needs a Net+ Certified technician.

  o Human Resources will now look for applications with the appropriate letters. Other applicants might have years of experience working on servers. Their resumes might also list every item on the job announcement. Human Resources often look at hundreds of resumes per day, however. In fact, some companies have "Optical Character Recognition" (Often called "OCR" software which reads over all the resumes as they arrive via e-mail or posted to a job website. Human Resources attempts to be as efficient as possible, so they will only respond to those resumes which have the "Certification Letters" they were anticipating.

Examples of International Network Technology Certifications:

There are a number of certifications which are international (Valid all over the world). The certifications of these types were created by large organizations and professionals in the field of network technology. Information combined from full-time professionals, educators, and technicians was combined to create the "The Handbook of Occupational Job Titles". This document is used to identify definite and specific tasks a "Network Technology" specialist would have to perform and have knowledge. Some certifications are "vendor neutral"

(Used for multiple companies and technologies) while others are "proprietary" (Offered exclusively by a specific company or organization). In order to gain industry certification, it is often required that a person pass some number of examinations or assessments hosted by the organization which sponsors the specific certification. Your desired area specialty in network technology will define which certification might be the most advantageous for you to attain. Some certifications which were active at the time of writing this book are as follows:

- **Net+ (Network+)** = Offered by a worldwide organization known as "CompTIA (Computer Technicians International Association). The Net+ often viewed as a "survey" certification. The primary focus of the certification is "Concepts and Knowledge". The certification examination assesses multiple terms existing in network technology from the perspective of many different devices from multiple companies. The examination does not focus on any single technology or process from start to finish. This is often viewed as the "Entry Level" network technology certification.
- **CCT (Cisco Certified Technician)** = Introduction Certification highlighting support and maintenance of routers and switches. Persons with this certification can use the Cisco Internetwork Operating System and the Cisco Command Line Interface (CLI). Classification of IP Addressing, subnetting and security are also aspects of this certification.
- **CCENT (Cisco Certified Entry-Level Networking Technician)** = These professionals have the ability service and maintain small enterprise networks and have a familiarity with basic network security. Objectives for this certification include network technology fundamentals, security and wireless concepts, routing and switching. The exam for the CCENT is also 50% of the exams required for the CCNA certification.
- **CCNA (Cisco Certified Network Associate)** = This certification is designed to assess the skills of Network Administrator and Engineers with 1-3 years of experience. The objectives of the exam(s) include the ability to configure, operate and troubleshoot various network technologies in a medium to large sized network environments. To gain this certification, it is possible to take either one exam or a two-part exam (Passing the first exam renders a person a CCENT, passing the 2nd exam will render a person also a CCNA.

- **MTA (Microsoft Technology Associate also known as an "MCP" – Microsoft Certified Professional)** = This certification is sponsored by Microsoft and based on networking software implementations. A person attempting an MTA would be well versed in "Operating Systems". Options for MTA at the time of writing this book included Windows 10, Server 2012, SQL Server, Exchange 2016, etc. Objectives for MTA-related examinations include assessing a person's understanding of network topologies, hardware, protocols, services and the OSI Model.

- **MCSA or MCSE (Microsoft Certified Solutions Associate and Microsoft Certified Systems Engineer)** = These certifications are achieved when a person takes 4 or more certification examinations in a specific order. The collections of exams include higher-order functions of the Windows operating system including aspects such as: Active Directory, Domain Name System, Group Policy, Remote Access, VPN's and Data Security and many other network services.

How to earn a Network Technology Certification:

There are many certifications which indicate various levels of knowledge in Network Technology. This text seeks to offer the foundation knowledge which would supplement a program of study for those desiring to achieve some of those network technology certifications. At the time of the writing of this book, the following are some of the certifications available in the field of network technology:

- **Self-Study and Simulators:**
  - In order to get certified, there are no mandated courses, colleges or training programs. In fact, many certified people have never taken a computer class. Essentially, they were "Self-Taught" after locating resources which would allow them to accumulate the knowledge to pass specific certification examinations. Suggested resources would be the following:
    - Simulators = These are practical software tools which allow practicing many high-order tasks required on network technology. There is no "best" software for each has features which might be advantageous for some certifications while not necessary for others. Some simulation software titles would include the following:
      - Virtual PC (Microsoft.com)

- Hyper-V(Microsoft.com)
- Virtual Box (Oracle.com)
- ➢ Certification Textbooks = These are produced by many different publishers. The book you are presently reading is actually an example of the type used to earn certification. Due to the many authors in computer technology,...it would be difficult to say which book is the "best" but there are some methods you can use to select the books which are best for your certification endeavors. The following are a few ideas:
  - Talk to technology professionals who have certifications. They can tell you which books and/or simulation software they used to pass the exams.
  - As "technology training" programs which books they use. Often time you can purchase the books without taking the classes.
  - Certification Organization Websites (i.e., "Comptia.com", "Microsoft.com" and "Cisco.com" often have links to books recommended for certifications. Be sure to check which numbers are associated with each exam prior to purchasing the books. Often books are sold which are associated with "old" and "Outdated" exams which are still using the same name.

- **Network Technology Training Schools:**
  - o Presently, there are many "For-Profit" institutions which have training programs and even degrees advertised as either "Network Technology Certificates" and even "Network Technology Degrees". Often times, these schools are called "Career Training Education (CTE)" institutions. These programs possess a broad variety of learning objectives and standards. When selecting a network technology program, do research on what standards they use to create the program. Questions such as the following would be beneficial when evaluating a potential program:

> What colleges or universities will accept the classes and credits from this program?
> What is the cost for this program compared to other schools both "For-Profit" and "Not-For-Profit"?
> What standards were used to establish the program?
> What organizations accredit the program?
> Please show me your job placement statistics?
> Am I allowed to re-take classes for free after completion of the program to keep skills up to date?

- **Two and Four-Year Colleges and Universities:**
  o Over the last 10 years, many colleges and universities have created "Network Technology" programs. The advantage to these colleges is that they also confer college degrees which would make a person more marketable in the technology field. In addition, having a degree allows a person to apply for other jobs outside of the field of network technology if they decided to change careers or needed employment until that perfect "Technology" job becomes available.

There are many institutions available which offer outstanding training experiences. Their costs range from free to extremely expensive, however. Do your research and balance out elements such as your available time and finances. Often times, certificate programs are a good place for basic understanding with the expectation that industry wide certification may follow in the future.

Recommendation on Correct Order to Take Certification Examinations:

Although it is not a requirement, having more than one certification is highly advantageous to a network professional. Multiple certifications will show perspective employers that a technician is an expert in many areas. If a technician had both a MCP and a CCENT, they know this person can both create a network and repair all the computers which are attached to the network. Many persons in the network technology field have a perspective on which examinations should be taken first and the particular order in which they should be attempted. There is no concrete document for most certifications attempts but there are some practical theories on the process. When planning on which certification(s) to take and their correct order,..give thought the following:

- **What jobs do you have interest?** = If a person wants to work on networks and has no desire to repair computers,..there is no need to take the A+. Simply stick with examinations such as "Net+", "CCENT", etc.
- **Which certification will make later certifications easier to achieve?** = Many certifications have similar objectives. Examples of similar test objectives would be such as the following certifications which all have similar questions:
  - **Net+**
  - **CCT**
  - **CCENT.**

Taking the examinations which have similar subject matter will make future examinations easier. It is like studying once to pass three different tests. There is no definite order of examinations at the lower levels of certification. Simply select the exams that will benefit you the greatest in the smallest amount of time.

Network Technology Groups and Organizations:

In addition to the specifics and details of connecting servers, there are a number of "theories" and "Concepts" which are not "hands-on" elements. Prior to many of the technologies used in network design, there were many groups and organizations which discussed methods of communication, terms and standards. Many of these organizations are the primary contact point for network technologies and many of their discussions have become the standards used worldwide. The following terms reflect some of the groups and theories which are highly utilized and well known in the field of network technology:

- **RFC** = (Request for Comments) is the general name for a document which is disseminated and discussed by multiple groups and organizations. These organizations are normally international and reflect primary groups of representatives in various areas of technology. Examples would be the Institute of Electrical and Electronics Engineer (IEEE) and the International Organization for Standardization (ISO). Each organization modifies the document, adding and subtracting statements, descriptions and categories. After an agreed amount of time, the organizations vote on the RFC and it is adopted as a "Standard". A "Standard" is a recommendation on how a product, function or activity should occur. It is not a legal rule, simply a guideline implemented to increase clarity and to reduce the amount of documentation which would have to accompany a product. The guidelines are then published by groups such as the Internet Engineering Task Force (IETF) and the Internet Society (ISOC), two of the primary organizations which establish standards for internet and computer technology communications. Some examples of RFC's include the following:

Request for Comment Examples	
RFC 20	ASCII format for network interchange
RFC 1518	Address allocation with CIDR
RFC 1542	DHCP/BOOTP complient routers
RFC 792	Internet control message protocol
RFC 1034	Domain names - concepts and facilities
RFC 1058	Routing information protocol
RFC 1459	Internet relay chat protocol

- **ISO** = (International Organization for Standardization) is an independent, non-governmental international organization based in Geneva, Switzerland. The participants of the ISO are considered to be experts who share knowledge and develop voluntary international standards to support innovation, consistency and global solutions to various worldwide situations. The members include over 161 national groups who all discuss, devise and develop standards for products, services and systems concerning quality and safety. There are over 21,000 International Standards and related ISO documents ranging from technology, food, energy, waste and many other areas. There are two primary models of communications in networking which are advocated by the ISO:

  - **OSI Model (Open Source Interconnect)** = A conceptual description listing the elements of network devices and how they communicate. This model separates network communication, software and devices into 7 distinct layers. Each layer supports specific functions which in turn allow transition into layers either above or below it. Without going into detail, the following are the seven layers of the OSI model and some of the related features within the layer:

OPEN SOURCE INTERCONNECT (OSI-MODEL)				
LAYER#	NAME	FUNCTION	ASSOCIATION	PDU TYPE
7	APPLICATION	File transfer, e-mail	Browsers ms-outlook	DATA
6	PRESENTATION	Formats data for transfer	Ansi, oem, etc.	DATA
5	SESSION	Creates and coordinates connections between applications		DATA
4	TRANSPORT	Data flow and error correction	Tcp, udp	SEGMENT
3	NETWORK	Establishes communication path between nodes	Routers	PACKET
2	DATA	Conversion to bits	Switches	FRAME
1	PHYSICAL	Carries the bits	Hubs, nic's, cables	BIT
WAYS TO REMEMBER LAYERS ORDER (First letter of each word represents layer:				
ALL PIMPS SELECT THE NICE DIAMOND PIECES				
ALL PEOPLE SEEM TO NEED DATA PROCESSING				
PLEASE DO NOT THROW SAUSAGE PIZZA AWAY				

- o **TCP/IP Model (Originally called the DOD model)** = This communication model separates network communications into 4 layers. Essentially, this model predates the OSI model and did not originally include much "software" related specifications (In the 60's, there were no applications such as "Firefox" and "Microsoft Word" so most communication technology was related to hardware). As time progressed, layers representing software were encompassed in the higher levels of the TCP/IP model. Below is a representation of the TCP/IP model as related to the OSI model:

TCP/IP MODEL		
LAYER#	NAME	FUNCTION
4	APPLICATION	FTP, Telnet, e-mail, DNS
3	TRANSPORT (HOST-TO-HOST)	Formats data for transfer
2	INTERNET	Creates and coordinates connections between applications
1	NETWORK	Data flow and error correction

How Does a Person Get Software?

How Does a Person Get Software?

In the field of server technology, it is important to practice using various types of software. Normally, there are many options available for companies such as Microsoft, Oracle and even Apple. When a person training is a student, the options are extremely large. Essentially, many companies will provide software to students for free or at an extremely reduced price. I know of students who were able to acquire fully-functioning versions of almost all of the Microsoft Office Suite as well as many of the server and workstation related operating systems at no cost to them. The first thing someone might think is that the software is "Pirated" (Essentially stolen without paying for it). Please relax. This is not case with the software I mention. The software is fully legal and obtained from the original vendor such as Microsoft. How are the students able to acquire the software, you ask? Really simple,..Microsoft wants you to sell it for them!

Essentially, Microsoft will provide specific applications and operating systems to a student enrolled in any college or training institution. The primary requirement is to register with an e-mail account which reflects an approved existing educational facility. Microsoft is allowing students to acquire applications and operating systems at no charge in order to increase their potential for future sales. The philosophy is that if students learn how to use Microsoft based applications and operating systems,..in the future that student might gain a job in which they can make recommendation of what software to purchase for the company of which they are employed. Most people purchase software that they are experienced with using. In the event that you have been using Microsoft Office products for three or four years,..there is a great potential that you will recommend the purchase of the same software in the future. In this process,..Microsoft may have given a student a software package which costs $300.00. If that same student who has now graduated,..purchases the software for 10 people in a company. Microsoft will now earn $3,000.00. This has been a marketing strategy Microsoft has used for over 10 years and it is one of primary reasons Microsoft Word is used by so many companies.

There are a number of websites which offer access to applications and operating systems. Some are what are called "Third-Party Vendors" (Not the original company which created or owns the software as opposed to companies such as Microsoft and Apple). The following are some of the websites which provide access to software as of the publication date of this textbook:

- **Microsoft Downloads** = https://imagine.microsoft.com/en-us/catalog

Let's Talk about Printers!

Let's Talk about Printers!

Although printers are not required discussion for a "Server" related textbook. It is necessary to list some aspects of them as they related to installation on a Windows Server. There are many types of printers such as "Ink Jet", "Laser", "Plotter" and many more. The focus for this item is general methods to connect a server to a printer. The following are some terms relative to adding a printer to a computer:

- **Printer Driver** = This terms represents the software required to allow an operating system to communicate, manage and control a printer. Some printers have drivers already installed in the Windows operating system so there is no need add any software. This is primarily the case when using a "USB" connected printer. Other printers which have a number of advanced options may require the use of installation media included with the printer packaging (Often a DVD or must be downloaded from the manufacturers website).

- **Shared Printer** = After a printer is installed, it is possible to allow many devices to access the printer. When a printer is shared,..other devices can "Browse ("Look around") to locate any shared printers. More capable computer technicians can use a "UNC" method and access the printer from another computer.

- **Local** = This term indicates that the printer is literally directly connected to the computer which is using the device. This direct connection can be parallel or USB. This is the primary method of printer installation on most personal windows computer.

- **Network Printer** = This indicates that there is a type of network in which the printer is "free standing" without a direct connection to any specific computer. The printer has a method of advertising its presences and allowing devices to connect, install drivers from the printer and utilize it to submit documents for printing. The connections for network printers very from Wireless, Bluetooth, Infrared and wired IP address. In large corporate environments, there may actually be a Windows Server which is in charge of dozens of printers. In this way,..specific users can be given access or denied access to specific printers. It is also possible to change the order of printing documents, clear documents that are not being printed or just deleting un-wanted print jobs.

Define "Software/Hardware Requirements".

Define "Software/Hardware Requirements".

When installing software on computers, it is very important to know the capabilities of that computer. Questions concerning how much RAM the computer can use,..what type of video card is installed and other issues such as hard drive space, operating system, etc. Installing an incompatible operating system on a computer is normally a fatal operation which can result in the loss of important data or the entire functioning ability of the computer. In order to compensate for this,..all software comes with two lists which outlines what a computer will need to run the software. The list comes in two forms:

- **Minimum Specifications** = These standards will allow the installation of the software with some limitations or restrictions. The limitations and restrictions could be the speed in which the software will operate or specific tasks which may be unavailable. If it is "video editing" program which allows new sounds to be recorded,..it would require a microphone of some type. If the computer has no microphone, the other functions of the software will still operate, but no live recording will take place. In addition to not being able to perform specific operations, other functions and processes could take minutes (Or literally "hours") to complete due to limited RAM or CPU capabilities. Adhering to the "Minimum Specifications" often results in poor performance and dissatisfaction in the software (Or the computer).

- **Recommended Specifications** = These are the standards which were used to test the software in various stages of its development. In addition, when using the recommended specifications, results, times, and expectations have been confirmed. Exceeding the recommended specifications often have the benefit of greater enhancement of the software. When working on businesses and corporate servers,..it is always best practice to exceed the recommended specifications.

Computer Network Terms and Protocols.

Computer Network Terms and Protocols:

Regardless of what type of computer is on a network, there must be software to allow it to be managed and to allow it to communicate. The software for computer communications is referred to as a "Protocol" (Best definition is simply an "Agreed method of communication"). The names of some of these protocols are often used to describe what makes up the primary communication standard for computers on both small business networks and networks as large as the internet. The following protocols and terms are highlights of the software's which allows computers to communicate:

- **WWW (World Wide Web)** = The term "Internet" is now used synonymously with WWW but there is an essential difference. Think of the "Internet" as a "large book" with many pages and chapters. World Wide Web (or "WWW") is the "Table of Contents" used to locate the specific item in the book in which a person has interest in researching. This term describes a searchable information storage system which includes entries from all over the earth. The items in the information system could be as small as two or three sentences on a document to as large as books with thousands of pages. In addition to text-based information this global information resource includes videos, music, graphics and interactive systems used for both knowledge, education and entertainment. Some of the earliest implementations of the World Wide Web are attributed to the work of Tim Berners-Lee as recently as 1989. He compiled code which allowed access to the global bank of knowledge known as WWW via using code such as HTML (Hypertext Markup Language), URLs (Uniform Resource Locators) communication protocols such as HTTP (Hypertext Transfer Protocol) and internet browsers (Netscape Navigator, Internet Explorer, Mozilla Firefox and Google Chrome).
- **URL (Universal Resource Locator) FQDN (Fully Qualified Domain Name)** = Method of typing a name in the address bar of a browser to locate a website (i.e., Netflix.com)
- **NetBIOS (Network Basic Input/Output System)** = This protocol which allows software on computers to exchange information a local area network (LAN). Client identities are identified using alpha-numeric identities (0-9 and A-Z). Often identities were limited to 8 characters or less.
- **NetBeui (NetBIOS Extended User Interface)** = This is an older protocol used for DOS and original Window networks (Primarily Windows 3.10

and Windows 95) designed for a single LAN segment. The protocol will not allow communications between discontinuous networks.

- **WINS (Windows Internet Name Service)** = This associates NetBIOS names to IP addresses on a LAN. This software was run as a service on a server to allow clients to locate other clients which might be on other LAN segments. WINS alone is non-routable but the software can be "carried" within another protocol such as networks that use NetBIOS over TCP/IP (NetBT).
- **TCP/IP (Transmission Control Protocol/Internet Protocol)** = Method for communications between computers on small and large networks. The protocol is actually a combination of two protocols suites verbally separated for easier explanation. Each suite is a combination of protocols but they have the same purposes as in the following:
    - **Transmission Control Protocol (TCP)** = Attempts to assure the dependable transmission of data between networks and devices. Within this capacity, the protocol will attempt to correct for data errors and requests re-transmissions of lost data.
    - **Internet Protocol (IP)** = Attempts to define the path that data, signals, packets, pdu's, etc., will take to travel between a sending device and destination.
- **IPv4 (Internet Protocol Version 4)** = The primary protocol in data communication over different kinds of networks. This protocol identifies computers by a 12 character decimal identity separated into 4 sections (192.168.1.1). Using this system allowed a worldwide network with over four billion IP addresses. With the increase of internet-connected devices (i.e., cell phones, car and home security, etc.) however, there is the potential of running out of IP's which can be accessed over the internet. Due to the address limitation, computers presently use other identity methods including IPv6, CIDR and VLSM (Terms will be explained and described later in this text).
- **IPv6 (Internet Protocol v6)** = This utilizes a combination of 32 hexadecimal characters for the identity of computers. An example of an IPv6 identity would be "fe80::75ea:6ec0:e6f8:f037". This method allows close to 340 undecillion available IP addresses. IPv6 also understands communications from IPv4 devices. Unfortunately, IPv4 devices cannot understand communications directly from IPv6 networks unless there is a software or device between the different networks to provide data conversion.

- **DHCP (Dynamic Host Configuration Protocol)** = This protocol gives identities to computers in the form of an IPv4 address. The protocol will also provide network settings so computers can find networks outside of the specific LAN. DHCP also attempts to assure that duplicated IP addresses are not given out to multiple computers which could cause an entire network to stop functioning.
- **DNS (Domain Name System (or Service or Server))** = This associates domain names into IP addresses. Whenever someone wants to go to "Disney.com" the request goes to DNS servers around the world. Those servers have a "Shared list" which includes all known domains linked to IP addresses. Once the domain is found in the DNS server, the IP address is sent to the computer which requested the domain. The computer then uses that address to get to the desired domain.
- **FTP (File Transfer Protocol)** = This is used to move files between computers. This is what occurs in the background when photos or other files are posted to online services such as "Facebook" or "ITunes". This is a robust protocol which checks each "part" of a file to make sure the total file has no errors in transmission.
- **HTTP (Hypertext Transfer Protocol)** = This allows computers to display text, graphic images, sound, video, and other multimedia files on applications known as "Browsers" (i.e., Internet Explorer, Chrome, Safari, etc.).
- **HTTPS (Hypertext Transfer Protocol Secure also called "Secure Sockets")** = This is used for sensitive data and transactions such as billing, credit cards transactions, user login and many other processes where security of data is required. The protocol "scrambles" the data being transmitted so it is difficult to read if captured by some other device or person. In addition, it attempts to create a more dedicated private connection between a user's web browser and the web server. Often times, HTTPS can be combined with many other security options such as web or e-mail certifications.
- **RDP (Remote Desktop Protocol)** = This allows a user to access a system without the need for being physically in the same location as the device. It is often used by various tech support services. Essentially, a person can sit anywhere in the world and interact with a computer as if they were setting directly in front of the computer. This protocol also enables a number of features of assistance to most computer or servers interaction such as the following:
  - ➢ Mouse and keyboard

> Data encryption
> Audio, printer and file redirection
> Clipboard sharing between a remote server and a local client

What is a Client Computer?

A "Client" performs all of the functions of a "Workstation" with a few special modifications. A "Client" requests services, access, or permissions from another computer called a "Server". Essentially, a client computer must ask a "Server" for approval for many of the functions a user might attempt on that client. For example,...many clients require a user to input a "username" and "Password" prior to using the client. When the username and password are typed by the user and the "enter" key is pressed,..that information is sent to a "Server" for approval. If the Server has knowledge of the username and password combination, a message is sent to the "client" approving the user and then the user's computer will activate. If the user does not exist, or if the user's account is turned off,..a "deny" message is sent to the client which prohibits the user's access to the computer. The following are other services a client must request:

- Connection settings for a business network.
- Access to the internet.
- Permission to access printers.
- Permission to access files on computers.
- Access to secured databases.

What is a Server?

In network technology, a "Server" is a system that "Gives out Stuff" or "Approvals". There are many types of servers in operation such as the following:
- DHCP Servers giving network configurations for workstations, phones and laptops.
- Web servers which hold and display websites.
- Video Services which allow access to movies online.
- Email servers for transmitting and receiving texts and documents.
- Security Servers which allow user access via usernames and passwords.
- Domain Name Servers which allow users to find internet websites using a friendly name.

What is an Operating System?

What is an Operating System?

This is the software which allows control and modification of hardware on computerized devices. To use the human body as a comparison, the operating system is like the "spirit" which guides activities or the "unconscious" functions such as breathing, eye blinking or heartbeat. Operating systems are always working anytime a computer is turned on, regardless if a person is interacting with the unit. Although there are many operating systems in existence today,..some of the most well-known are **Unix, Microsoft Windows, the Mac OS and Linux.**

The operating system performs functions such as moving data between parts inside the computer such as the hard drive, RAM and or the internet connection. Every activity which can be performed is executed by the operating system. Every time a key is pressed, the operating system performs actions. All programs (Also called "Applications") are also maintained and controlled by the operating system allowing each of them to share data streams and storage space. All data stored on a computer is arranged by the operating system as well as communicating with parts outside of the computer such as speakers, monitor and printer. The operating system also provides a method for a user to interact with the computer called a "User Interface (Also called "UI")". The User Interface on most computer have various names such as GUI (Graphical User Interface), WebUI (Web User Interface) and CLI (Command Line Interface). The discussions within this text will include aspects of all three methods.

Windows Graphical Users Interface (GUI).

Windows Graphical Users Interface (GUI):

In the early 1980's it was required for computer operators to always have an understanding of the storage method used by a computer. Today, most users of Windows computers have no idea that there is a thing called an "operating system" which is arranged like a file cabinet with many "drawers" holding "directories" which also hold "sub-directories" which end with a collection of "files". This method of organizing data and programs on computers is called a "Directory Structure".

```
C:\csu>tree
Folder PATH listing for volume Windows
Volume serial number is 00000051 A866:6146
C:.
├───Server 2012
├───software
│   ├───CodePics
│   ├───NetSimK
│   │   └───CiscoSem2Intro
│   ├───OFFICE03
│   │   ├───FILES
│   │   │   ├───ACCRT
│   │   │   ├───OWC10
│   │   │   ├───OWC11
│   │   │   ├───PFILES
```

Oftentimes, the training for operating computers became an issue so computer programmers began to investigate methods to make interacting with a computer less complicated. After years of experiments, operating systems began to come with the ability to perform CLI commands without every knowing any of them. This revolutionary method of communicating and controlling with computers became known as using a Graphical User Interface (Often abbreviated in writing as "GUI" and verbally by using the word "Goo-ey").

In many cases, computer users no longer had to even use the keyboard. Depending on the computer being used,..most of the daily required functions could now be performed by simply using a mouse and "clicking" on a picture on the display. These "pictures" are now referred to as "Icons" or "Buttons". The total collection of items which can be utilized makeup a "Graphical User Interface (Known as a "GUI" and usually pronounced as "Goo-ey"). The GUI was created to remove the need to know CLI commands to activate and operate computer systems. Using a GUI allows symbols called "icons" on a computer screen to be activated via clicking a mouse or keyboard button. These icons are directly associated with commands which are run in the background by the operating system. In addition, many commonly used functions can be displayed on a "menu" screen via clicking additional buttons on a mouse. In the world of Windows Computing, the following are items used by many computer operators:

- **Desktop** = This is the primary area to access programs when a windows computer boots. It includes many icons which activate programs as well as sections which display active programs, present time and date, volume controls and many other features convenient for users. The desktop can also be "personalized" for a user to display favorite photos, websites, weather displays, calendars, and many other items.

- **Start Menu/Button** = This is the core area to locate and activate programs on a computer. Recently used applications, newly installed programs and a feature which allows a user to search for files exist in this area. With the advent of Windows 8 and 10, the "button" aspect of this area has many different styles which can be activated. This "Shell" in the illustration is only one of the many. In addition, there are also technical-related icons such as the command line interface, Windows Help and Support and System tools.

- **Search Programs and Files (Also called the "Run" option)** = Originally, this area allowed a technician to utilize CLI functions, one of those being searching the operating system for files lost by a user. As time progressed, Microsoft noticed non-technical users often performed the function of searching for files so they enhanced the area to allow faster and more efficient searches for files based on name, date of creation, size of file, type of file and many other attributes. The original technical functions are still enabled in this area however, so programs can be launched or network resources can be typed in various formats such as using a "UNC".

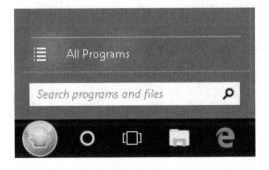

- **Recycle Bin** = This area is the default place which stores files if they have been deleted from other areas of the computer. Think of it as a "safety feature" in case you accidently delete a file and later decide you needed. If a file is deleted, it literally stays in this area until about 85% of the actual space on a computer's hard drive (Area which stores files long-term) is used,..then data in the Recycle Bin will begin to erase files, starting with the older files first.

- **Task Bar** = This is the bar which appears at the bottom of most Windows desktops. It displays shortcuts for often used programs, programs active on the computer, network connections, volume controls, calendars, and many other items. Although traditionally at the bottom, the Taskbar can be moved around to any edge of the display and also resized or hidden from view. The Taskbar can also be "personalized" with icons, widgets and gadgets.

- **Windows Explorer (Displays Directories or "Folders")** = This interface allows a GUI display of the directory (Often called "Folders" in GUI terms) within a computer system. The interface has many display options such as mini-pictures of photos called "Thumbnails", "Date of Creation", "Large Icon", "File Preview" windows, and many more. The Explorer window can also be re-positioned, and resized for better view of items contained within the present window.

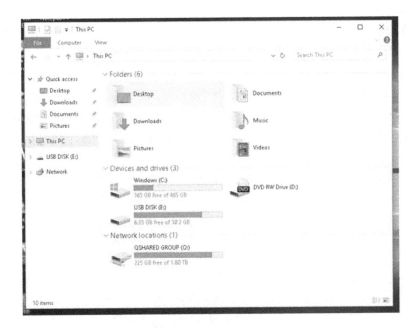

- **Title Bar** = This area identifies the application presently active as well as the name of the directory being viewed. The Title bar is found both in the windows operating system as well as many programs. It also possible to use the Title Bar to reposition the entire window of a program or directory in a different location on the desktop in the event the view of another window is obscured.

- **Sizing Buttons** = These icons appear on the far right of a title bar. They are control features which allow you to quickly alter the characteristics of a displayed window. The following are the functions of each button:
  - **Minimize** = Will shrink an entire window and only display its presence on the Task Bar. To return the window to its previous size and location, the icon representing the minimized window need only be "double-clicked".
  - **Restore (Full or Down)** = Depending on the previous stage of an explorer window, this button provides two functions. Either it will make the window encompass the entire area available for display on a monitor or the button will return window taking up the entire display to the previous size and location on the desktop.

- **Exit/Close** = Depending on the window in which the buttons are located,..this icon will either remove one active document from a number of documents running in an application from view, or totally turn off a running program.

- **File Menu** = These icons appear as "words" beneath the Title bar and above the detail area of most explorer windows. Each icon gives access to command menu's relevant to whichever explorer window to which it is associated. In the window displayed, you see the options "File", "Computer" and "View". The File menu options will change depending on the window or the application. When using the present version of Microsoft Word, the File Menu reads "File", "Insert", "Page Layout" and a few more items particular to that application.

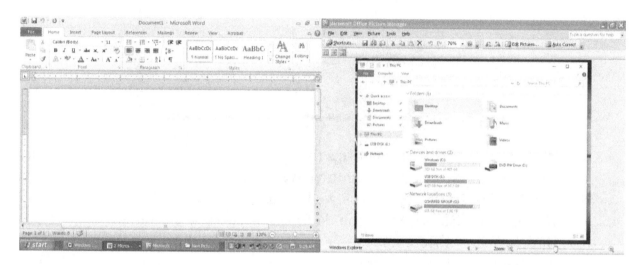

- **Control Panel** = This area allows access to devices, programs, customizations and system settings for the operating system. It is possible from here to configure network settings, power settings and many more features. Another aspect is to use this area to establish security, anti-virus and system update settings.

- **Computer Management** = This is a well-known interface created by Microsoft to allow a technician quick access to a number of operating system controls. There are hundreds of controllable aspects of a Windows computer. Computer Management allows you to both view and customize different elements of a computer's environment.

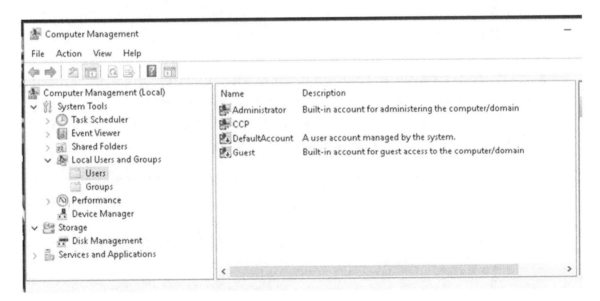

- **MMC (Microsoft Management Console)** = This is a control interface which allows a user to create a Control Interface with particular selected Snap-ins and Extensions. Actually, "Computer Management" is actually an MMC which was customized by Microsoft. Many technicians create their own MMC Snap-ins they routinely use on computers during repairs.

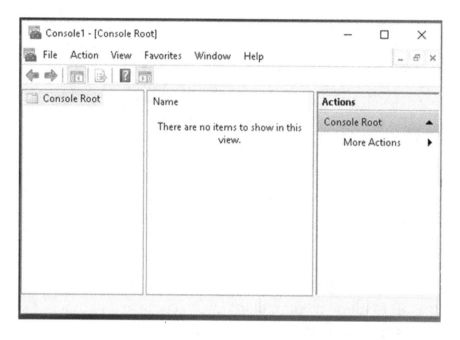

- **MMC Snap-In** = This is a term used to describe the control interfaces which appear in an MMC such as Computer Management. The items such as "Local Users and Groups", "Services" and "Shares" are just a few of the many. Various Snap-ins can be loaded into most MMC's.

- **MMC Extension** = In relation to an MMC, an extension is the end of a Snap-in. It is the place of the interface in which there are no additional sub-features. An example of a Snap-in would be "Services". Many different Snap-ins have a multitude of Extensions.

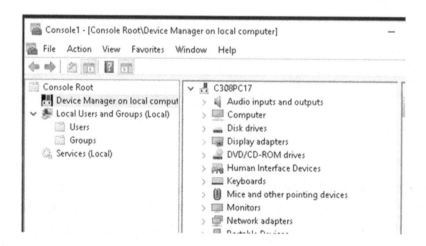

- **Local Users and Groups** = This is a common feature within Computer Management. This allows the creation of different users on a single computer. This gives the benefit of allowing each user to have their own "design" to the Desktop area as well as creating different sections for users to store their documents, pictures and other files. Within "Local Users and Groups" some users (Such as "Parents") will be "in charge" of the computers and can make any changes possible. Other users (Such as "Children") should be prohibited from making changes. In order to accomplish this, there are "Groups" setup on most operating systems. Group names and abilities include the following:
    - **Administrator** = Total control of the computer system.
    - **User** = Only offers ability to use programs but not make any system-wide changes.
    - **Power User** = Allows minor changes to computer which will not affect the overall function of the operating system.

The Command Line Interface (CLI).

The Command Line Interface (CLI):

This is an interface which requires an in-depth understanding of the structure of operating systems. In order to activate elements and functions in the operating system, a user is required to type out the exact word which initiates a function. Spelling must be perfect in order to manipulate a CLI operating system. Many present day operating systems offer access to the CLI. On Windows-based operating systems the CLI is often confused with an operating system which is no longer used called "DOS (Short for "Disk Operating System"). Below is an example of using a CLI to ascertain the network settings being used by a computer.

```
C:\>ipconfig

Windows IP Configuration

Ethernet adapter Local Area Connection 3:

        Media State . . . . . . . . . . . : Media disconnected

Ethernet adapter Local Area Connection 5:

        Media State . . . . . . . . . . . : Media disconnected

Ethernet adapter Wireless Network Connection 6:

        Connection-specific DNS Suffix  . :
        IP Address. . . . . . . . . . . . : 192.168.1.152
        Subnet Mask . . . . . . . . . . . : 255.255.255.0
        Default Gateway . . . . . . . . . : 192.168.1.1

C:\>
```

One of the most misunderstood options available on operating is entitled **the "Command Line Interface"** normally abbreviated as "CLI". Many persons who have some knowledge of computers will refer to this access method as "DOS". The "look" of "DOS" and the "CLI" are very similar. Below is a DOS screen. Notice the top does not have a title bar.

```
C:\>
```

Notice that when using the Windows CLI, there is a Title Bar at the top:

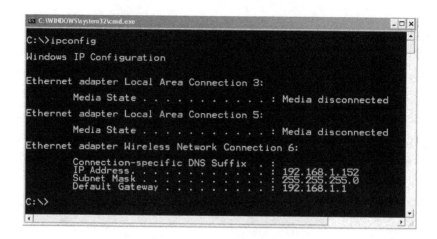

"DOS (Disk Operating System)" is an extremely outdated operating system used by Microsoft between 1980 and 1998. Essentially, the operating system DOS used "command-words" to perform functions. If a user did not understand the correct format for the "words" they would be unable to utilize a computer. About 1993, one of the first GUI's (Graphical User Interface) entitled "Windows for Workgroups", was produced. This GUI was installed on top of DOS which allowed functions to be performed using pictures referred to as "icons" and "buttons". The buttons interacted with DOS as a control feature. DOS was replaced by Windows 98 but the ability to use command line was retained using the command "command" and/or "cmd" in the "Search" field of a "Start Menu". Most technicians referred to the "search" field as the "Run" option.

In the field of computer/server technology, there are many CLI functions used. One of the reasons which supports CLI functions is that the command words do not often change. The "buttons" and "icons" normally change between operating systems or even between different versions of the same operating systems. The command "ping" for example is the same on Linux, Unix, Windows and even the Cisco Router and Switch operating systems. All are run from a CLI. The following are some of the more well-known CLI commands performed on Windows:

- **Dir** = Displays the contents of the directory presently being viewed.
- **Cls** = Removes previous command results from the CLI.
- **Cd** = Redirects the focus of the command prompt (i.e., "C:\Windows\System32>") to a directory within the present directory.
- **cd** = Redirects the focus of the command prompt (i.e., "C:\Windows\System32>") to the root (Top) of the drive being viewed.
- **cd ..** = Redirects the focus of the command prompt (i.e., "C:\Windows\System32>) back one level to the previous or containing directory.
- **Mkdir <name>** = Creates a directory that is named in the command.
- **Rmdir <name>** = Eliminates a directory that is named in the command.
- **Notepad** = This command will open up the program "Notepad".
- **Calc** = This command will activate the Microsoft Calculator (If it is installed).
- **MSPaint** = This command will activate Microsoft Paint (If installed).
- **Tree** = This command will display the relationship between directories and subdirectories in a linked-line format **(Notice: The results of this command could take a few minutes to complete).**
- **"Tree /p" or "Dir /p"** = Displays a few lines of the results of the command with a pause. Pressing any key on the keyboard will allow the display of files and directories to continue with pauses until the complete results of the command are complete.

The following are some practical applications of some CLI commands. All start with accessing the run option in "Search Programs and Files". Many of the examples listed will be evaluated later in this book. Feel free to experiment with them before the listed exercises, they will not damage your computer. Although, you might want to do them on a computer that is not important because it will reduce the computers security:

- **Running a program like "notepad":**
  - ➢ C: (Make the CLI concentrate on the "C:\>")
  - ➢ CD\ (Makes the CLI concentrated on the Root of the directory.)
  - ➢ Notepad (Starts the Notepad application)

- **Running a program like the Windows "Calculator":**
  - ➢ C: (Make the CLI concentrate on the "C:\>")
  - ➢ CD\ (Makes the CLI concentrated on the Root of the directory.)
  - ➢ Calc (Starts the "Calculator" application").

- **Creating a new directory called "Staff" inside of "C:\>" drive:**
  - ➢ C: (Make the CLI concentrate on the "C:\>")
  - ➢ CD\ (Makes the CLI concentrated on the Root of the directory.)
  - ➢ Mkdir staff

- **Connecting to a shared directory entitled "staff" on a computer called "Server01":**
  - ➢ C: (Make the CLI concentrate on the "C:\>")
  - ➢ CD\ (Makes the CLI concentrated on the Root of the directory.)
  - ➢ Net Use X: \\Server01\Staff

- **Setting an IP address of "172.16.20.10" on an interface with a subnet mask of 255.255.255.0:**
  - ➢ C: (Make the CLI concentrate on the "C:\>")
  - ➢ CD\ (Makes the CLI concentrated on the Root of the directory.)
  - ➢ netsh interface ipv4 set address name="3Com19111" static 172.16.20.10 255.255.255.0

- **Restarting a Computer:**
  - ➢ C: (Make the CLI concentrate on the "C:\>")
  - ➢ CD\ (Makes the CLI concentrated on the Root of the directory.)
  - ➢ Shutdown /r (Turns off the system after all processes normally close)

- **Shutting down a Computer:**
  - ➢ C: (Make the CLI concentrate on the "C:\>")
  - ➢ CD\ (Makes the CLI concentrated on the Root of the directory.)
  - ➢ Shutdown /s (Turns off the system after all processes normally close)

Open a CLI on your system and attempt the above commands. None of the commands listed above will damage a computer. In addition, there are some exercises you can do using CLI which might assist in repairing or servicing a computer or server in the future.

Utilizing "Batch Files".

Utilizing "Batch Files":

In computer technology, there are a number of methods performing tasks and actions. Methods of turning on programs vary between different applications and tasks. The most commonly used method of activating programs presently is using "icons" or "buttons" on the start menu or desktop area. What is not well known is that each button executes dozens of actions on the CLI of the operating system. It is possible to combine hundreds of commands and have the all performed by using a click on an icon which is associated with a file launched by a single word input in the operating systems CLI. The process of using a single file to perform multiple tasks is often called "Scripting". "Scripting" comes in a large variety of formats ranging from "Visual Basic (VB)" and "Java Script". In the area of network technology and computer repair, the script type called "Batch Files" are often used.

Batch files can be used to allow a computer or application to perform a number of commands after a user has activated a single file. The file extension for a batch file is "<filename>.BAT". The file might be activated by using an icon or using a command thru the CLI. When using the CLI, there is a requirement to making the command usable from various areas. The following are options for running a batch file from the CLI (Note: These options are mentioned for reference but not utilized in this text).

Execute the command from the same directory in which the batch file exists. Create or modify a file called the "Autoexec.bat" to load the directory path of the batch file into memory upon computer startup. If there was a batch file called inside of a number of sub-directories entitled "getpay.bat" it would be possible to place the following statements within the autoexec.bat in order to utilize the command from any CLI location:

- **Path=C:\myscripts\mybatches ("Getpay.bat" is located inside of this directory.)**

The following is a task which could be performed by the batch file. The file has the purpose of connecting to a server and activating a file called "Payroll.xls":

- **C:** (Make the CLI concentrate on the "C:\>")
- **CD** (Makes the CLI concentrate on the Root of the directory.)
- **Net Use X: \\Server01\Staff** (Connects the present operating system to a directory entitled "Staff" within a server called "Server01").

- **X:** (Make the CLI concentrate on the "X:\>")
- **CD staff** (Makes the CLI concentrate on the directory "staff".)
- **Payroll.xls** (Opens the file which now displays on the computer which activated the batch file).

Introduction to PowerShell.

Introduction to PowerShell:

PowerShell is a command-feature in Windows operating systems. The type of commands used are "commandlets" (CMDLET's) and many server professionals advocate the use of PowerShell as opposed to a GUI. Although PowerShell accompanies any installation of Windows Server, some servers use only PowerShell Commandlets when Windows Server has been installed as a "Core" installation which does include a GUI (Graphical User Interface). Installing Windows Server "Core" has some advantages such as the following:

- **Additional Storage Space** = The GUI files which create the "icons", "Windows", "Desktop", "Snap-Ins", etc., require storage on a large amount of the hard drive space. A Windows server "Core" installation does not require those files which allows the storage space to be used for other programs and files. If there is ever a need to utilize a GUI on the "Core" server, a different computer can be used to access the core server "remotely" and display the normal GUI interface. In addition, the GUI can also be installed at any time thru adding additional features (Of course,…an administrator would have to start the process using PowerShell.

- **Server Security** = Due to there being no graphical user interface,..the only way the server can be controlled is with exact commands for every function applied in the PowerShell CLI. The number of persons proficient in PowerShell commands is far less than those who only know how to manipulate servers via Snap-ins and Applets.

There are a large body of PowerShell commands available on the various versions of Windows Server Operating Systems. The totality of PowerShell is beyond the scope of this textbook. The following commands are some which may be used on Server Operating Systems to perform normal maintenance functions. In order to perform the commands and functions, it is required to have an operating Windows Server Domain Controller.

- **Access the PowerShell CLI:**

```
Administrator: Windows PowerShell                                  ☒

Windows PowerShell
Copyright (C) 2012 Microsoft Corporation. All rights reserved.

PS C:\Users\Administrator>
```

- **Command to display which Active Directory Services are presently installed on a Server:**
  - ➢ Get-WindowsFeature AD-Domain-Services

```
PS C:\Users\Administrator> Get-WindowsFeature AD-Domain-Services

Display Name                                              Name
------------                                              ----
[X] Active Directory Domain Services                      AD-Domain-Services
```

- **Command to create a user account for a user named "Chuck":**
  - ➢ New-ADUser Chuck

```
PS C:\Users\Administrator> New-ADUser Chuck
```

- **Command to display the properties for a user named "Chuck":**
  - ➢ Get-ADUser Chuck

```
Administrator: Windows PowerShell                                  ☒
PS C:\Users\Administrator> Get-ADUser Chuck

DistinguishedName : CN=Chuck,CN=Users,DC=Cool,DC=com
Enabled           : False
GivenName         :
Name              : Chuck
ObjectClass       : user
ObjectGUID        : e21b2672-9678-4fac-b0a6-77bc25a99389
SamAccountName    : Chuck
SID               : S-1-5-21-1008211405-1634479270-2939740301-1118
Surname           :
UserPrincipalName :
```

- **Command to create a new Active Directory Group called "SpaceDudes":**
  - ➢ New-ADGroup Spacedudes 1 (The digit 1 will place the group in the Default user's directory).

```
PS C:\Users\Administrator> New-ADGroup Spacedudes 1
PS C:\Users\Administrator> _
```

- **Command create a shared folder on a Server:**
  - ➤ New-Item "C:\MainOfficeShare" –type directory

```
PS C:\Users\Administrator> New-Item "C:\MainOfficeShare" -type directory


    Directory: C:\


Mode                LastWriteTime     Length Name
----                -------------     ------ ----
d----         6/8/2018   11:55 AM            MainOfficeShare
```

- **Command to display present network adaptor information:**
  - ➤ Get-NetAdapter

```
PS C:\Users\Administrator> Get-Netadapter

Name                      InterfaceDescription                    ifIndex Status       MacAddress
----                      --------------------                    ------- ------       ----------
Ethernet                  Intel(R) PRO/1000 MT Desktop Adapter         12 Up           08-00-27-47-84-89
```

- **Command to display network adaptor configurations such as IP address, Subnet Mask, etc.:**
  - ➤ Get-NetIPConfiguration

```
PS C:\Users\Administrator> Get-NetIPConfiguration


InterfaceAlias       : Ethernet
InterfaceIndex       : 12
InterfaceDescription : Intel(R) PRO/1000 MT Desktop Adapter
NetProfile.Name      : Cool.com
IPv4Address          : 172.16.10.10
                       10.10.10.10
IPv6DefaultGateway   :
IPv4DefaultGateway   : {10.10.10.1, 172.16.10.1}
DNSServer            : ::1
                       172.16.10.10
                       172.16.10.20
```

- **Command to set the following IP configurations on a server to 100.100.100.10 and Subnet Mask 255.255.0.0:**
  - ➤ Set-NetIPAddress -InterfaceIndex 2 -IPAddress 100.100.100.10 -PrefixLength 16

- **Command to remove the following IP configurations on a server (Note: If there is no additional ip addresses on the interface, the system will activate DHCP (Indicated by an APIPA address on the interface). Below is the readout before removing the ip address:**
  - ➢ Remove-NetIPAddress -IPAddress 192.168.0.1

```
                                          Administrator: Windows PowerShell
PS C:\Users\Administrator> Get-NetIPConfiguration


InterfaceAlias         : Ethernet
InterfaceIndex         : 12
InterfaceDescription   : Intel(R) PRO/1000 MT Desktop Adapter
NetProfile.Name        : Cool.com
IPv4Address            : 172.16.10.10
IPv6DefaultGateway     :
IPv4DefaultGateway     : 172.16.10.1
DNSServer              : ::1
                         172.16.10.10
```

After typing command, it will require confirmation for proceeding with the IP address removal:

```
PS C:\Users\Administrator> Remove-NetIPAddress -IPAddress 172.16.10.10

Confirm
Are you sure you want to perform this action?
Performing operation "Remove" on Target "NetIPAddress -IPv4Address 172.16.10.10
-InterfaceIndex 12 -Store Active"
[Y] Yes  [A] Yes to All  [N] No  [L] No to All  [S] Suspend  [?] Help (default is "Y"):
PS C:\Users\Administrator> Get-NetIPConfiguration


InterfaceAlias         : Ethernet
InterfaceIndex         : 12
InterfaceDescription   : Intel(R) PRO/1000 MT Desktop Adapter
NetProfile.Name        : Cool.com
IPv4Address            : 169.254.200.174
IPv6DefaultGateway     :
IPv4DefaultGateway     : 172.16.10.1
DNSServer              : ::1
                         172.16.10.10
```

- **Remove Default Gateway Setting:**
  - ➢ Remove-NetIPAddress -DefaultGateway 172.16.10.1
    - o After typing command, it will require confirmation for proceeding with the IP address removal:

- **Remove Domain Name Server Setting:**
  - ➢ Remove-NetIPAddress -DefaultGateway 172.16.10.1
    - o After typing command, it will require confirmation for proceeding with the IP address removal.

Nodes, Clients, Identities and Character-Types.

Nodes, Clients, Identities and Character-Types:

Depending on which protocol or software is used on a network, devices can be identified many different ways. The following methods are ways in which servers display their existence as well as what can be used for communications between devices (Note: Regardless of the naming convention, many characters are not compatible with many names such as "spaces" between characters and some special symbols such as " \ " or " * "):

- **Hostname** = Using Alpha-Numeric characters (A-Z and 0-9). Examples would be "PC_17", "Dad_Computer", "Room_012" etc. This type of name is totally arbitrary and can be changed. A simple view of a hostname can be displayed on Windows systems by typing in "hostname" and pressing "enter" when using a CLI.

- **IP Address (Decimal)** = Characters are numeric (0-9) and are arranged in four sections separated by decimals (.) called "Octets". In addition, the primary numbers used in IPv4 networks are between 0 and 255 in each section. Examples are "192.168.1.10" or "169.254.101.20". IP address arrangements appear in many network-related settings on computers, cell phones, televisions, etc. This type of identity can randomly change depending on how the network interface is configured. A simple view of an IP address can be displayed on Windows systems by typing in "ipconfig" and pressing "enter" when using a CLI.

- **Mac Address (Hexadecimal)** = Also called a "Physical Address" and uses a limited arrangement of Alpha-Numeric characters including only 0-9 and A-F (There are other hexadecimal character combinations but the ones listed are used in network technology). Usually arranged in three groups of four characters separated by decimals or six groups of two characters separated by hyphens (-). Examples would be A9-6F-CE-AA-87-99. The mac-address is actually encoded in the network interface of a device. It is globally unique and more like a server's "fingerprint". This identity is configured to be permanent and can only be changed by persons with higher levels of electronics, programming or cyber-security experience. A view of a devices physical address can be displayed on Windows systems by typing in "ipconfig /all" and pressing "enter" when using a CLI.

- **Binary** = Binary characters are the foundation of computer and software technology. These characters are represented with either a "0" or a "1". Combinations of binary characters cause actions in software, hardware and identify devices. Often with programming, the two options for bits have specific meanings as in the following:

- o **0 = off, no or false.**
- o **1 = on, yes or true.**
- o Total numbers of combined characters have meaning in elements of instruction, storage and/or speed. Specific well known combinations have the following names:
  - ➢ **Bit** = Single character as in "0" or "1".
  - ➢ **Nibble** = Four bits as in "0000" or "1111" or "0101".
  - ➢ **Byte (Sometimes called an "Octet")** = Eight bits, or two nibbles as in "11110000"

What is a "MAC Address"?

When working in the field of network technology it is required to understand at least three identities which servers can use to identify themselves and to be contacted. Those identities are as follows:

- **Hostname** = Appears as a simple word such as "PC1" or "MyComputer".
- **IP address** = Decimal Identity such as "172.16.20.1"
- **MAC Address** = Combination of letters and decimal numbers such as "A8-45-CD-23-FA-BE"

In our present discussion, we will evaluate "MAC Addresses". MAC (Often stands for "Media Access Control") Address. This identity is one the most essential of server identities. Many people compare the Mac Address to a human "finger print". This collection of letter and numbers are globally unique. Essentially, this means that there should be no duplicated Mac address on any server in the world when the device is produced by a manufacture. A Mac address is programmed into a ROM chip that is part of the servers' "network interface card (NIC)". If the NIC is ever moved to another network device (i.e., "Out of one server and inserted into a different server.") the MAC will follow the NIC and now be part of the server of which it is inserted.

Because the code for the MAC is part of a piece of hardware, we often refer to it as a "Physical Address". In order to view a computers MAC you would utilize the command "IPCONFIG /ALL" such as in the following example:

```
C:\WINDOWS\system32\cmd.exe                                           _ □
        Description . . . . . . . . . . . : 3Com EtherLink XL 10/100 PCI For Com
plete PC Management NIC (3C905C-TX) #4
        Physical Address. . . . . . . . . : 00-50-DA-5F-77-0C

Ethernet adapter Wireless Network Connection 6:

        Connection-specific DNS Suffix  . :
        Description . . . . . . . . . . . :
        Physical Address. . . . . . . . . : EC-1A-59-B0-B6-DD
        Dhcp Enabled. . . . . . . . . . . : Yes
        Autoconfiguration Enabled . . . . : Yes
        IP Address. . . . . . . . . . . . : 192.168.1.152
        Subnet Mask . . . . . . . . . . . : 255.255.255.0
        Default Gateway . . . . . . . . . : 192.168.1.1
        DHCP Server . . . . . . . . . . . : 192.168.1.1
        DNS Servers . . . . . . . . . . . : 192.168.1.1
        Lease Obtained. . . . . . . . . . :
        Lease Expires . . . . . . . . . . :

C:\>
```

When servers communicate, although IP addresses are configured, most communications occur using the MAC address of the computer. This is because the MAC address is more dependable. The other two identities on servers (i.e., "Hostname" and "ip address") can be easily changed. MAC addresses do not change (Except when a computer uses a "flash update" for repairs or participates in "Spoofing" to attempt to compromise a network). MAC addresses are a total of 12 characters normally separated into groups of two such as the following:

- **CC:CC:CC:MM:MM:MM**
- **CC-CC-CC-MM-MM-MM**

When initial communications occur between servers and other network devices, particularly inside a specific LAN, the IP addresses between nodes are used. After a successful communication of some sort occurs,...the devices exchange MAC addresses. This allows faster and more stable communications due to a table being used called "ARP (Address Resolution Protocol). The ARP table is created as successful communications are established between computers. To witness the processes of servers using ARP and MAC addresses for communication, the following utilities can be used:

- **Arp –a** = This command shows all the IP addresses and MAC associations known by a computer. Some may be "dynamic" (Subject to change) while others will be "Static (Will not change)"
- **Arp –d *** = This command clears all IP address to MAC associations.
- **Nbtstat –w.x.y.z** = Command will display all identities associated with an IP address in the Arp Table.

IP Addressing Versions and Concepts.

IP Addressing Versions and Concepts:

Regardless of the type of software used or the type of servers they all require identity information. We discussed the following identities in the section "Nodes, Clients and Identities". Different protocols use many different identities for communication but for our discussions we will primarily discuss "IP Addresses". The following areas will be the focus of the discussion of this book concerning IP addresses:

- **IP version 4** = One of the primary standards established by ARPANET for network identities on the internet. Although worldwide organizations formally established it in the mid-1980's, IPv4 routes much Internet traffic today and will more than likely exist for quite some time. Elements which allow IPv4's continued existence is in the elements that it is a widely used protocol in data communication and allows compatibility across a number of different network types. Multiple types of servers support IPv4 and there are many features such as "Dynamic Host Configuration Protocol", "Vender Class" and many other utilities. IPv4 is a connectionless protocol which means that the source and destination does not have a dedicated connection but uses intermediary devices to transmit data in a "Relay-Race" fashion". It provides the logical connection between servers by providing identification for each device. Due to this configuration, there is a possibility of failed delivery or even duplicated data being sent. Although the protocol has errors inherent in its composition, higher level protocols protect against errors. IPv4 uses a 32-bit (four-byte) method allowing for a total of 2^32 addresses (just over 4 billion addresses). The addresses are converted from binary to decimal when displayed for better understanding for humans. Because of the demand of the growing Internet, the available numbers of remaining addresses were nearing exhaustion anticipated between 2004 and 2011. The problem concerning "lack of available network addresses for the internet" was foreseen many years prior which gave rise to other methods of network addressing for the internet.

- **IP Version 6**= Internet Protocol version 6 (IPv6) is the version of the Internet Protocol (IP) initiated for use near the year 2011 which provides an identification for servers, routers and servers system across the Internet. IPv6 was developed by the Internet Engineering Task Force (IETF) to address the foreseen exhaustion of available of IPv4 addresses. IPv6 uses a 128-bit address which provides for 2^28 which is a number so large it is said to be an "Undecillion". IPv6 addresses are represented as eight groups of four "Hextets" or "Hexwords" separated by colons such as in the example;

- o "2001:1234:abcd:9944:c6750:cf00:36bb:94ee".
  - ➤ The example given in the previous sentence is called "uncompressed" although many times, the full address can be compressed by eliminating groups of zero's.

- **Classfull IP addressing** = Primary method used on the Internet from 1981 to about early 1990's. Using the Classfull method, address spaces are divided into five address classes of "A, B and C" with two more of "D" which is for "multicasting" and "E" reserved for military and experimental purposes. Below is an example of Classfull IP addressing:

Traditional Classfull IP Address Standards			
Class	Leading Octet	Subnet Mask	Maximum Hosts
A	0-126	255.0.0.0	16,777,214
B	127 - 191	255.255.0.0	65,534
C	192 - 223	255.255.255.0	254
D	224 - 239	Multicast	NA
E	240 - 247	Military Use	NA
*Note = This displays the maximum "Usable" hosts and not the pure mathematical derivatives.			

- **Classless IP Addressing** = Due to the growth of the internet, there was a need to extend the range of available addressing. IPv6 is a method but the primary restriction to it is that older IPv4 devices could not communicate using IPv6. A solution to the decreasing number of available IPv4 addresses was produced with the implementation of CIDR and VLSM:
  - o **Classless Internet Domain Routing (CIDR)** = When networks were developed, traffic was routed based on matching Classfull IP Classes (i.e., "A, "B", "C", etc.) with a specific subnet mask ("255.0.0.0", "255.255.0.0" or "255.255.255.0"). Due to the increase in the number of devices, classfull IP addressing could not support the number of routes on the internet. IPv6 was created, but IPv4 will not understand routing from IPv6. Due to this challenge, programmers began to re-compile server operating systems to utilize the "binary" form of numbers as opposed to the traditional method of "decimal" utilization. Because of this enhancement, subnet masks can include the following new octets: 128, 192, 224, 240, 248, 252, and 254. These new octets are combined with traditional IP addresses as in the examples below:

CIDR Examples	
Host IP	Subnet Mask
204.16.10.54	255.255.255.128
199.240.78.95	255.255.240.0
224.16.76.81	255.255.255.192

Netmask Conversions		
Binary	Octet	CIDR
10000000	128	/25
11000000	192	/26
11100000	224	/27
11110000	240	/28
11111000	248	/29
11111100	252	/30
11111110	254	/31
11111111	255	NA (Or /32)
Assumes 1st three octets of "255.255.255.x"		

> Although decimal numbers are displayed, the arrangement of the "Binary "0's" and "1's" dictate network parameters such as:
> ❖ Number of networks
> ❖ Number of hosts
> ❖ Paths between networks

> **Variable Length Subnet Masks (VLSM)** = Paralleling the utilization of CIDR, the method of documenting IP configurations has also evolved. As opposed to using decimal numbers, the amount of "1's" in "binary" are added up and a decimal number is used to reflect the total written at the end of an IP address after a "/" character (Often called a "forward slash"). Take the following for example:
> ❖ Traditional subnet mask = 255.255.255.128

1) Binary format
   11111111.11111111.11111111.10000000
2) Count number of binary "1's" = 8+8+8+1 = 25 total.
3) VLSM documentation = /25

- o **Reserved Addresses** = When using IPv4, IPv6 or CIDR, specific types of IP addresses have special uses. We often call these addresses "Reserved" or "Special Use". Regardless of their use, they both have one common element. Reserved IP addresses are not to be used on devices directly connected to the internet (On the Department of Defense backbone). If reserved IP addresses are used on devices which are directly connected to the internet backbone, the situation will result in the device not communication or a conflict with other devices on the internet. The following are some of the "reserved" addresses:
  - ➤ **169.254.X.Y** = Network systems will self-assign an address within in this range if a DHCP server cannot be contacted.
  - ➤ **192.168.X.Y** = Often used for private networks or training purposes.
  - ➤ **127.0.0.1** = This is called the "loopback" and "localhost" address. This address is used as a utility to ascertain if a server's interface can be contacted by the rest of the network. The loopback is often used if the servers IP address is hidden. Using a "ping" command, a technician can perform the following to test if the server he or she is working on can be contacted by other devices.
  - ➤ Some other reserved IP address appear in the chart below:

Reserved/Special Use IP Addresses
10.0.0.0 – 10.255.255.255
172.16.0.0 – 172.31.255.255
192.168.0.0 – 192.168.255.255
127.0.0.1 - 127.255.255.254

Parts of an IP Address:

Based on the communication requirements on a network, various methods of node identification can be used (As in the prior mentioned methods of "hostname", "physical address" and/or "IP address", etc.). When using IP addresses, specific sections of an address have terms which are used to describe their purpose.

- **Network Address/ID** = The section of an IP address which all nodes on a section of a network have in common. Often times, it is the leading numbers on an IP address leading from left to right. An example would be 209.15.X.Y subnet mask of 255.255.0.0. The first two octets identify the network address (Traditionally, the section of the subnet mask will give an idea of the network address because whichever octet section used by the network address ID will reflect the same number of "255's" in the subnet mask.
  - Think of it like a "last name" on a family. There could be multiple people in a family. Such as the "Smith" family. All of the people in the family could be referred to as "the Smith" family. A network or network section uses the network address and it is common on all computers such as in the "Branch Office" network.

- **Host ID/node ID** = Section of an IP address which is unique for individual systems. This would be like the "first name" of all the people in the "Smith" family. There could be "Bob Smith", "Sam Smith" and "Sally Smith". In reference to a network, think of the following computers:
  - 172.16.10.10 = Part of the "172.16.10" network but the host ID is "10".
  - 172.16.10.15 = Part of the "172.16.10" network but the host ID is "15".
  - 172.16.10.20 = Part of the "172.16.10" network but the host ID is "20".

When there are subnets which need to function with other subnets, somewhere on the network there must exist a routing device of some type. Before discussion and attempting labs in subnetting, the following is a brief review about IP types:

- **Classfull IP addressing** = Primary method used on the Internet from 1981 to about early 1990's. Using the Classfull method, address spaces are divided into five address classes of "A, B and C" with two more such as "D" which is for "multicasting" and "E" reserved for military and experimental purposes. Below is an example of Classfull IP addressing:

Traditional Classfull IP Address Standards			
Class	Leading Octet	Subnet Mask	Maximum Hosts
A	0-126	255.0.0.0	16,777,214
B	127 - 191	255.255.0.0	65,534
C	192 - 223	255.255.255.0	254
D	224 - 239	Multicast	NA
E	240 - 247	Military Use	NA
*Note = This displays the maximum "Usable" hosts and not the pure mathematical derivatives.			

- **Classless IP Addressing** = Due to the growth of the internet, there was a need to extend the range of available addressing. IPv6 is a method but the primary restriction to it is that older IPv4 devices could not communicate using IPv6. A solution to the decreasing number of available IPv4 addresses was produced with the implementation of VLSM and CIDR.
    - o **Classless Internet Domain Routing (CIDR)** = When networks were developed, traffic was routed based on matching Classes (i.e., "A, "B", "C", etc.) with a specific subnet mask ("255.0.0.0", "255.255.0.0" or "255.255.255.0"). Due to the increase in the number of devices, classfull IP addressing could not support the number of routes on the internet. IPv6 was created, but IPv4 will not understand routing from IPv6. Due to this challenge, programmers began to re-compile server operating systems in a manner which utilizes the "binary" form of numbers as opposed to the traditional method of "decimal" utilization. Because of this enhancement, subnet mask octets can include the following 9 numbers: 0, 128, 192, 224, 240, 248, 252, 254 and 255. With this method, the arrangement of "0's" or "1's" which are the "Binary" version of the decimal numbers dictate the following:
        - ☐ **Number of Networks**
        - ☐ **Number of Hosts**
        - ☐ **Routing Paths**

    - o **Variable Length Subnet Masks (VLSM)** = Paralleling the utilization of CIDR, the method of documenting IP configurations has also evolved. Utilizing terms such as "Class A, B or C" or the traditional subnet masks such as "255.0.0.0, 255.255.0.0 and 255.255.255.0" are often replaced with the following class "C" CIDR examples:

Netmask Conversions		
Binary	Octet	CIDR
10000000	128	/25
11000000	192	/26
11100000	224	/27
11110000	240	/28
11111000	248	/29
11111100	252	/30
11111110	254	/31
11111111	255	NA (Or /32)
Assumes 1st three octets of "255.255.255.x"		

o As opposed to using decimal numbers as the subnet mask, the total amount of "binary" 1's" in the subnet mask are added together and a two character decimal number is used to reflect the subnet mask after the IP address and a "/" character (Often called a "forward slash"). Take the following for example:
   □ Given CIDR subnet mask = 255.255.255.128
      ➤ Binary format 11111111.11111111.11111111.00000000
      ➤ Count number of binary "1's" = 8+8+8+1 = 25 total.
      ➤ VLSM documentation = /25

IP version 6 Format and Structure:

The display of an IP version 6 address uses what is known as "hexadecimal" characters. These characters include the alpha-numeric values of "A, B, C, D, E, F" and "0, 1, 2, 3, 4, 5, 6, 8 and 9". Remember that any character viewed in a character format is only for the human eye. Computers actually use the "binary" equivalent any displayed character. Below are the listed hexadecimal characters associated with their binary equivalence:

Network Related Numbers Conversion		
Decimal	Hexadecimal	Binary
0	0	0000
1	1	0001
2	2	0010
3	3	0011
4	4	0100
5	5	0101
6	6	0110
7	7	0111
8	8	1000
9	9	1001
10	A	1010
11	B	1011
12	C	1100
13	D	1101
14	E	1110
15	F	1111

Let's look at the various formats and displays of the IPv6 format and characters. IPv6 addresses are written as a string of hexadecimal values. Take the following for example: 2001:1234:EF00:5678:9AAC:DDEE:FF11:ABCD

- Written in full form displays 32 hexadecimal characters.
  - o Every 4 bits = Single hexadecimal character.
- Total bits length is 128.
  - o Display is separated into eight sections separated by colons.
    - Example as in = x^1:x^2:x^3:x^4:x^5:x^6:x^7:x^8.
    - Each "x" = 16 bits in or four hexadecimal characters often called "Hextet" or "Hexword"

How DHCP Allocates Addresses (In Brief):

Often times, there are hundreds of computers which require addresses on a network. Not only is it an immense task to manually configure each computer, but there is a great possibility that duplicate addresses will be applied to multiple computers which can hamper and even disable entire networks. Due to this requirement of networks, there are methods in which clients can receive an address from a server normally called a "DHCP" or "BOOTP" server. DHCP is an abbreviation for "Dynamic Host Configuration Protocol. "BOOTP" is an older method of tracking and distributing addresses and will not be illustrated in this text. A DHCP device or "Server" can be an operating system on a computer or simply a device which performs the addressing function. For our discussion, we will concentrate on the DHCP Server function implemented in Windows Server Networks as they relate to network clients.

On most computer networks, when clients are turned on, they have no IP address settings. During their boot-up, they will advertise their existence with what is called a "Broadcast" which is a "Scream to the Network" that the device would like an IP address given to it. The broadcast is associated with the "physical" or "MAC" address of the device (i.e., "3D-44-AC-FC-55-66"). Often the "broadcast" address appears in the following forms (In IPv4 and Hexadecimal):

- "0.0.0.0"
- "255.255.255.255"
- "FF-FF-FF-FF-FF-FF"

The signal is "heard" by a "DHCP" server which in turn, sends an IP address to the client by using the "physical" address as the target. Once the client agrees to use the offered IP address, the DHCP server records the address as given out and will not use it again until the client no longer requires the address, such as when the computer is turned off. The default time that is often set on Windows clients is about 8 days, but this time can be shortened or lengthened. In addition to an IP address, the client is also given the following network settings (May be more or less depending on the network):

- **Subnet Mask**
- **Domain Name**
- **Default Gateway location.**
- **Domain Name Server location.**

Oftentimes, a device will fail at receiving an IP address for a multitude of reasons. Using CLI commands, it is possible to ascertain if a network device was unsuccessful in IP attainment. Using the normal utility "ipconfig", if the address appears with the first two octets of "169.254.x.y" and a subnet mask of "255.255.0.0" the following is assumed:

- **The computer is connected to a network.**
- **Electronically, the network card interface and all associated cables are connected.**
- **The client was not able to receive and address from a DHCP server.**

The ip address of "169.254.x.y" is defined as "APIPA" (Automatic Private IP Addressing). This is the result of the process of a network device giving itself an IP address due to inability to communicate with a DHCP server. Prior to assigning itself an IP address, the client will use "ICMP" (Internet Control Messaging Protocol) to "Ping" an IP address it desires to use in the "169.254.x.y" range. If no other device responds, the client will use the address. "Ping" is a CLI network utility often used in network troubleshooting. The command will display if a specific network device has the ability to be contacted. The format to use the command is as follows:

- **Ping <ip address of target network device>**

Below is a display of a ping when a device is successfully contacted. Depending on the operating systems, successful detection of a network device will render 3 to 8 "positive" replies.

```
Command Prompt
Microsoft Windows [Version 10.0.14393]
(c) 2016 Microsoft Corporation. All rights reserved.

C:\Users\c308>ping 10.10.41.76

Pinging 10.10.41.76 with 32 bytes of data:
Reply from 10.10.41.76: bytes=32 time<1ms TTL=128
Reply from 10.10.41.76: bytes=32 time<1ms TTL=128
Reply from 10.10.41.76: bytes=32 time<1ms TTL=128
Reply from 10.10.41.76: bytes=32 time<1ms TTL=128

Ping statistics for 10.10.41.76:
    Packets: Sent = 4, Received = 4, Lost = 0 (0% loss),
Approximate round trip times in milli-seconds:
    Minimum = 0ms, Maximum = 0ms, Average = 0ms
```

If a device is not located, the following would be the response:

```
C:\WINDOWS\system32\cmd.exe
C:\>ping 57.32.54.99

Pinging 57.32.54.99 with 32 bytes of data:

Request timed out.
Request timed out.
Request timed out.
Request timed out.

Ping statistics for 57.32.54.99:
    Packets: Sent = 4, Received = 0, Lost = 4 (100% loss),

C:\>
```

Many times, network technicians require more than 3 to 8 responses regardless of if they are positive or negative. In this situation, a "switch" to the "ping" option is utilized which will cause the ping to continue until manually terminated (Often called an "extended" or "infinite" ping). To terminate an extended ping, the control key combination "Ctrl+C" must be performed. The format and an illustration are as follows:

```
C:\WINDOWS\system32\cmd.exe

C:\>ping 98.139.180.149 -t

Pinging 98.139.180.149 with 32 bytes of data:

Reply from 98.139.180.149: bytes=32 time=34ms TTL=50
Reply from 98.139.180.149: bytes=32 time=46ms TTL=50
Reply from 98.139.180.149: bytes=32 time=34ms TTL=50
Reply from 98.139.180.149: bytes=32 time=51ms TTL=50
Reply from 98.139.180.149: bytes=32 time=46ms TTL=50
Reply from 98.139.180.149: bytes=32 time=26ms TTL=50
Reply from 98.139.180.149: bytes=32 time=21ms TTL=50
Reply from 98.139.180.149: bytes=32 time=26ms TTL=50
Reply from 98.139.180.149: bytes=32 time=33ms TTL=50
Reply from 98.139.180.149: bytes=32 time=24ms TTL=50

Ping statistics for 98.139.180.149:
    Packets: Sent = 10, Received = 10, Lost = 0 (0% loss),
Approximate round trip times in milli-seconds:
    Minimum = 21ms, Maximum = 51ms, Average = 34ms
Control-C
^C
C:\>_
```

Process to Manually Configure an IP Address (On Windows Systems):

Depending on the device or operating system, in order to communicate with other network devices there is the requirement for settings which allow transmission and reception of signals. In order for this to occur, devices have to share methods of communications commonly referred to as protocols. There are multiple protocols used in present network technology. The discussions in this text will primarily revolve around the protocol classified as TCP/IP (Transmission Control Protocol/Internet Protocol). This method of communication has two presently utilized version of version 4 and version 6. Much of our discussion will relate to version 4. In addition, many of the sections discussed will be directly related to Microsoft Operating Systems as well as the Cisco IOS.

When utilizing Windows operating systems in network environments, there are both GUI and CLI methods of viewing and manipulating network configurations. When using CLI, the command prompt is activated and then we will use the command IPCONFIG. When using this command in its smallest format, the CLI displays basic network settings.

```
 C:\WINDOWS\system32\cmd.exe                                          _ □ ×

C:\>ipconfig

Windows IP Configuration

Ethernet adapter Local Area Connection 3:

        Media State . . . . . . . . . . . : Media disconnected
Ethernet adapter Local Area Connection 5:

        Media State . . . . . . . . . . . : Media disconnected
Ethernet adapter Wireless Network Connection 6:

        Connection-specific DNS Suffix  . :
        IP Address. . . . . . . . . . . . : 192.168.1.152
        Subnet Mask . . . . . . . . . . . : 255.255.255.0
        Default Gateway . . . . . . . . . : 192.168.1.1

C:\>
```

When performing the basic command of IPCONFIG the following are explanations of the display:

- **IP Address** = Decimal identity of computer on a TCP/IP network.
- **Subnet Mask** = Provides segmentation of groups of computers.
- **Default-Gateway** = Point which allows a section of a network to communicate with devices outside of that network.

The command also has optional modifications available which will show more specific displays of network configurations or allow the use of advanced features and tasks. In order to use the enhanced features,.. additional words and characters must be appended to the command. The character which must be added is often called a "Forward Slash" or a "Switch" normally represented by using "/". The "Switch" is followed by a number of other commands which can perform a number of operations. The most common enhanced command is by adding the "All" perimeter. This command will display a complete readout of all the settings presently used by the windows client as follows:

```
C:\WINDOWS\system32\cmd.exe                                    _ □

C:\>ipconfig /all

Windows IP Configuration

        Host Name . . . . . . . . . . . . : 3Com
        Primary Dns Suffix  . . . . . . . :
        Node Type . . . . . . . . . . . . : Hybrid
        IP Routing Enabled. . . . . . . . : No
        WINS Proxy Enabled. . . . . . . . : No
        DNS Suffix Search List. . . . . . : router.home

Ethernet adapter Local Area Connection 3:

        Media State . . . . . . . . . . . : Media disconnected
        Description . . . . . . . . . . . : Realtek PCIe GBE Family Controller
        Physical Address. . . . . . . . . : 40-09-4F-06-09-DD

Ethernet adapter Local Area Connection 5:

        Media State . . . . . . . . . . . : Media disconnected
        Description . . . . . . . . . . . : 3Com EtherLink XL 10/100 PCI For Com
plete PC Management NIC (3C905C-TX) #4
        Physical Address. . . . . . . . . : 00-09-4F-5F-DD-09-4F

Ethernet adapter Wireless Network Connection 6:

        Connection-specific DNS Suffix  . : router.home
        Description . . . . . . . . . . . : Belkin USB Adaptor
        Physical Address. . . . . . . . . : EC-09-4F-B0-B6-DD
        Dhcp Enabled. . . . . . . . . . . : Yes
        Autoconfiguration Enabled . . . . : Yes
        IP Address. . . . . . . . . . . . : 192.168.1.152
        Subnet Mask . . . . . . . . . . . : 255.255.255.0
        Default Gateway . . . . . . . . . : 192.168.1.1
        DHCP Server . . . . . . . . . . . : 192.168.1.1
        DNS Servers . . . . . . . . . . . : 192.168.1.1
        Lease Obtained. . . . . . . . . . : Saturday, August 12, 2007 7:40:59 AM

        Lease Expires . . . . . . . . . . : Sunday, August 13, 2007 7:40:59 AM

C:\>_
```

IP addresses are essential in network communications on TCP/IP networks.
There are a number of methods utilized to establish address settings on servers.
The following are some of the options:

- **Static Address (Manual)** = This allows an IP address to be established by
  a technician. The technician can either use a CLI or GUI to manually type
  in an IP address. To set an IP address using CLI, the following could be
  done:
    - **netsh interface ipv4 set address name="3Com19111" static
      100.100.100.10 255.255.255.0 100.100.100.100**

The above command inserted "100.100.100.10" as the computer's IP address
with a subnet mask of 255.255.255.0 and a default-gateway setting of
100.100.100.100. To set an IP address using the GUI, the following would be
performed:

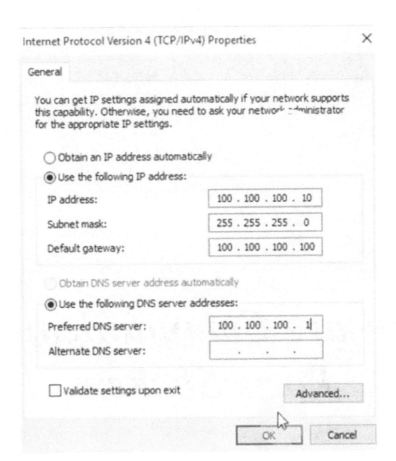

Software Communications Ports/Sockets.

Software Communications Ports/Sockets:

Earlier in this book, there is the mention of "protocols" which are simply "rules of communication" between network devices. Some of the protocols listed were "DHCP", "Telnet" and "HTTP". As long as network devices are using similar protocols, they will have the ability to communicate and/or exchange data. There are other elements related to network communications, however. These other elements are classified as "Ports".

"Port" is a term used to identify a logical, software path between devices. Whatever media (Cable, wireless, etc.) software uses to travel is not a single cable in function. In actuality, there are 65,535 different paths of communications available between any devices communicating on a network. The following diagram is an example using "DHCP", "HTTP" and "Telnet":

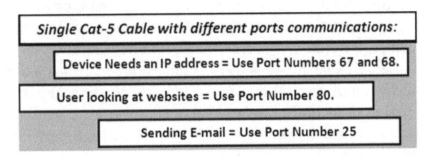

Any or all of these ports can be used at any given time. Different types of software are configured to communicate on different ports. The picture below displays different communications occurring on a computer which is presently viewing "Disney.com". The command used in the command line interface (CLI) after visiting the website is "netstat –a". There are a number of ports which display "Disney.com" related entries. Each of the entries which reflect "website" communications will display as an IP address with a "colon (:)" followed with "HTTP" and "HTTPS":

```
TCP    192.168.1.118:63508    server-54-192-36-235:http  LAST_ACK
TCP    192.168.1.118:63510    ec2-54-243-80-169:http   LAST_ACK
TCP    192.168.1.118:63511    server-54-192-36-125:http  LAST_ACK
TCP    192.168.1.118:63512    server-54-192-36-125:http  LAST_ACK
TCP    192.168.1.118:63513    server-54-192-36-125:http  LAST_ACK
TCP    192.168.1.118:63521    server-54-192-36-125:http  LAST_ACK
TCP    192.168.1.118:63527    server-54-192-36-235:http  LAST_ACK
TCP    192.168.1.118:63537    133:http                 LAST_ACK
TCP    192.168.1.118:63539    192.229.210.12:http       LAST_ACK
TCP    192.168.1.118:63540    ec2-52-27-8-169:http      TIME_WAIT
TCP    192.168.1.118:63541    ec2-184-73-198-200:http   TIME_WAIT
TCP    192.168.1.118:63545    ec2-52-205-153-11:http    TIME_WAIT
TCP    192.168.1.118:63546    ec2-54-88-194-5:https     ESTABLISHED
TCP    192.168.1.118:63547    192.229.210.12:http       LAST_ACK
TCP    192.168.1.118:63548    192.229.210.12:http       LAST_ACK
TCP    192.168.1.118:63550    ec2-54-88-194-5:http      TIME_WAIT
TCP    192.168.1.118:63552    a184-26-44-105:http       LAST_ACK
TCP    192.168.1.118:63553                              LAST_ACK
```

The Department of Defense (DOD) along with other agencies (i.e., InterNIC) support standard documentation to categorize which ports are used for specific communications. Many vendors have accepted agreements to create software for similar purposes to all communicate on the same port (i.e., web browser creators such as "Firefox", "Chrome" and "Internet Explorer" all use ports 80 and 443 for default website viewing). Other ports are also standardized for other uses which may periodically move to other ports. Since there are 65,535 ports, many are not identified for any particular use. Any port can be utilized at any time for any transmission type without any updates to any international standard documents. Due to the different elements involved in the use of different ports, there are terms which are used to describe the port categories along with their respective numbers as in the following:

Port Range	Category
1-1023 are	Well-known
49152-65535	Dynamic
1024-49151	Registered

Although specific ports are associated with particular function or software, it is possible to reconfigure software to utilize other ports. For example, "Telnet" uses port 23 while e-mail (SMTP) uses port 25. It is possible to configure telnet to test an e-mail server by making telnet use port 25. The process for testing an e-mail server is beyond the scope of this book, but it required mention for those who desire network certification. Often time on certification examinations, it is required to identify some specific ports and protocols within the "Well-known (Also called "Commonly Used")" or commonly used range. The table below displays many of the ports often manipulated in troubleshooting and or normally assessed on certification examinations:

Port	Protocol
20, 21	File Transfer Protocol (FTP)
23	Telnet
25	Simple Mail Transfer Protocol (SMTP)
53	Domain Name Server (DNS)
67, 68	Dynamic Host Configuration Protocol (DHCP)
69	Trivial File Transfer Protocol (TFTP)
80	HyperText Transfer Protocol (HTTP)
110	Post Office Protocol (POP3)
143	Internet Message Access Protocol (IMAP4)
443	HTTP with Secure Sockets Layer (SSL)
3389	Remote Desktop (RDP)

Character Conversion Tables.

Character Conversion Tables:

Many devices with one ID type must communicate with totally different device ID types. For this to occur, there is the need to convert between identities. For example, some situations require a binary identity to be displayed in decimal format. To understand this process, it is necessary to learn how to convert between the three following identities; decimal, binary and hexadecimal. A table which will be used a lot in this text is displayed below:

Network Related Numbers Conversion		
Decimal	**Hexadecimal**	**Binary**
0	0	0000
1	1	0001
2	2	0010
3	3	0011
4	4	0100
5	5	0101
6	6	0110
7	7	0111
8	8	1000
9	9	1001
10	A	1010
11	B	1011
12	C	1100
13	D	1101
14	E	1110
15	F	1111

There are many ways to convert numbers mathematically. When taking many certification examinations, calculators are not allowed and processing questions concerning math may result in a great loss of time (Most certification examinations have a specific time limit for completion). It is important to utilize a method which will render quicker results without the need for duplicated writing. In order to accomplish this goal, I (The writer) have created a "pointing table" which can expedite the process of number conversions as well as other related processes required in network technology and certifications. The writer has created a number of methods and tables which can assist the learning of conversions. One of the tables used is the "Decimal to Binary Conversions Table" displayed below:

Decimal to Binary Conversions							
128	64	32	16	8	4	2	1

- **Formula Legend:**
  1. **N1** = Original number.
  2. **R#** = Resultant number.

With the table above, it is possible to translate decimal numbers to binary and the reverse. No higher order math is necessary. Simply place numbers into the "value spaces" and either add or subtract depending on the desired operation. Using the table above, perform the following:

- **Convert the decimal number "3" into a binary value. Here is the overview:**
  1) Moving "left to right" indicate a binary "1" for any spot which can be subtracted from N1.
  2) Moving "left to right" indicate a binary "0" for any spot which cannot be subtracted from N1.
  3) When a number can be subtracted, do so and continue using the result (R#)

Let's work the problem:
- **Step 1 = Left to right, find the value spot which can be SUBTRACTED FROM "3" (N1).**
  1. The value spot "128" cannot be subtracted from "3".
     ➢ Place a "0" in the binary row beneath the value spot.
     ➢ Continue moving to the right.
  2. The value spot "64" cannot be subtracted from "3".
     ➢ Place a "0" in the binary row beneath the value spot.
     ➢ Continue moving to the right.
  3. The value spot "32" cannot be subtracted from "3".
     ➢ Place a "0" in the binary row beneath the value spot.
     ➢ Continue moving to the right.
  4. The value spot "16" cannot be subtracted from "3".
     ➢ Place a "0" in the binary row beneath the value spot.
     ➢ Continue moving to the right.
  5. The value spot "8" cannot be subtracted from "3".

> Place a "0" in the binary row. Continue moving to the right.

6. The value spot "4" cannot be subtracted from "3".
   > Place a "0" in the binary row beneath the value spot.
   > Continue moving to the right.
7. The value spot "2" CAN be subtracted from "3".
   > Subtract the value spot (2) from the original number "3".
   > We now using the remainder of "1" as the number we are evaluating.
      ❖ We call this "R1" (The digit changes based on what was left after subtracting the found number from N1).
   > Place a "1" in the binary row beneath the value spot.
   > Continue moving to the right.
8. The value spot "1" can be subtracted from "1" (R1).
   > Subtract the number in the value spot (1) from the result number "1"
   > We now using the remainder of "0" as the number we are evaluating.
      ❖ We call this "R2" (The digit changes based on changing resultants).
   > Place a "1" in the binary row beneath the value spot. The results will look like table below:

Decimal to Binary Conversions							
128	64	32	16	8	4	2	1
0	0	0	0	0	0	1	1
X	X	X	X	X	X	(-2)	(0)

9. Going from left to right, add up all the value spot numbers which have a "1" beneath them (2 + 1 = 3).
10. The binary equivalent of the decimal number "3" = 00000011.
    > Some books drop the zero's before the first 1 which makes the number display as "11". Don't be fooled. Always keep the zeros in mind!

Let's try another: Find the binary version of the decimal number 40. Remember the steps:

- Moving "left to right" indicate a binary "1" for any spot which can be subtracted from N1.
- Moving "left to right" indicate a binary "0" for any spot which cannot be subtracted from N1.
- When a number can be subtracted, do so and continue using the result (R#). In this case "N1" = "40"
    - Step 1 = Left to right, find the value spot which can be SUBTRACTED FROM "40" (N1).
        1. The value spot "128" cannot be subtracted from "40".
            - Place a "0" in the binary row beneath the value spot.
            - Continue moving to the right.
        2. The value spot "64" cannot be subtracted from "40".
            - Place a "0" in the binary row beneath the value spot.
            - Continue moving to the right.
        3. The value spot "32" CAN be subtracted from "40".
            - Subtract the number in the value spot (32) from the original number "40" (N1) leaving the first result of 8 (R1).
            - We are now using "8" as the number we are evaluating.
                - ❖ We call this "R1" (The digit changes based on changing resultants).
                - ❖ Continue moving to the right.
        4. The value spot "16" cannot be subtracted from "8".
            - Place a "0" in the binary row beneath the value spot.
            - Continue moving to the right.
        5. The value spot "8" CAN be subtracted from "8".
            - Subtract the number in the value spot (8) from the first result number "8" (R1) leaving the second result of 0 (R2).
            - We are now using "0" as the number we are evaluating.
                - ❖ We call this "R2" (The digit changes based on changing resultants).
            - Continue moving to the right.
        6. The value spot "4" cannot be subtracted from "0".
            - Place a "0" in the binary row beneath the value spot.
            - Continue moving to the right.
        7. The value spot "2" cannot be subtracted from "0".
            - Place a "0" in the binary row beneath the value spot.

▸ Continue moving to the right.

8. The value spot "2" cannot be subtracted from "0".

▸ Place a "0" in the binary row beneath the value spot.

9. Going from left to right, add up all the value spot numbers which have a "1" beneath them (32 + 8 = 4).

Decimal to Binary Conversions							
128	64	32	16	8	4	2	1
0	0	1	0	1	0	0	0
X	X	(-8)	X	(-0)	X	X	X

10. The binary equivalent of the decimal number "40" = 00101000.

▸ Some books drop the zero's before the first 1 which makes the number display as "101000". Don't be fooled. Always keep the zero's in mind.

Try a few of the numbers below on your own. Convert the following decimal numbers into binary:

1. 129 = Answer 10000001
2. 70 = Answer 01000110
3. 20 = Answer 00010100
4. 10 = Answer 00001010
5. 250 = Answer 11111010

How to Convert "Hexadecimal" to "Binary":

The characters include both reading letters and decimal numbers limited to "0 thru 9" and "A – F". Computers cannot process double-characters such as the number "13" or "10". In order to process double digit numbers for network technology (Or numbers higher than the decimal number "9") a letter was selected to represent certain numbers which have two digits. The following table show the numbers which are represented by each hexadecimal character:

Hex	Represents		
1	1		
2	2		
3	3		
4	4	A	10
5	5	B	11
6	6	C	12
7	7	D	13
8	8	E	14
9	9	F	15

Remember, computers only show letter and number characters so humans can understand the message. Computers and other servers have to use binary numbers. With hexadecimal numbers, each character is actually a representation of a collection of binary characters ("0's" or "1's"). Each character always represents four "bits" **(Called a "Nibble"). Understanding that a MAC has 12 hexadecimal characters, multiplying each character by "four bits" will render a total number of 128 bits**. These bits are what are used by computer hardware and software for functions. The hexadecimal readout is only so humans can better differentiate between different MACS. In the field of network technology, it is necessary to understand how binary collections create specific MAC addresses. To provide this function the following "Hex to Binary" table is used:

Hex to Binary Conversions								
A	8	4	2	1	8	4	2	1
B								
C								

Notice that the table is similar to the "Decimal to Binary" scale in which it has eight "value spaces" and it has three levels. The following are the functions of each level:

- **A-Level (Value Areas)** = Indicates 8,4,2,1-8,4,2,1
- **B-Level (Yes/No Area)** = Indicates if can be subtracted from hexadecimal character.
- **C-Level (Hex Character)** = Specific character being evaluated.

Using the table,..it is possible to convert between hexadecimal characters and their associated "nibbles" or binary equivalence. Using the table and a process, we can carry out the conversion using the following steps:
1. Locate a full 12-character MAC address.
2. Isolate the first set of Hex characters (Separated by " : " or " . ").
3. Locate the "Left-most" hex character in and place in "C=Left" of the conversion table.
4. Locate the "Right-most" hex character in and place in "C=Right" of the conversion table.
5. Subtract all "A-Row" numbers from the "C-Row" numbers from left to right.
6. All numbers you cannot subtract, record as a binary "0" in the "B-Row".
7. All numbers you can subtract, record as a binary "1" in the B-Row and retain remainder for next subtraction.
8. Continue until you have two complete "Nibbles" on the "B-Row".

Take the following example: Given the MAC address of 23-3C-DD-AB-FE-72, what is the binary version of the 2nd character set? Let's work the problem:
- 2nd character set = "3C"
- Place the characters on the conversion chart as in the following (Remember to convert "Letters" into corresponding "Numbers"):

	Hex to Binary Conversions							
A	8	4	2	1	8	4	2	1
B								
C	Left = 3				Right = C (12)			

- Begin the subtraction process on the "Left-Side" with the character "3":
  1. Ask the question "Is this a LETTER or a NUMBER?"
     ➤ If character is a LETTER use conversion chart to change to correlated number and go to step #2.

Hex	Represents
A	10
B	11
C	12
D	13
E	14
F	15

➢ If character is a NUMBER, continue to step #2.

2. Can you subtract 8 from 3 = No (Which is "0" in binary).
   ➢ Place a "0" in the "8-B" slot.
   ➢ Continue to next "A-Row" number.

3. Can you subtract 4 from 3 = No (Which is "0" in binary).
   ➢ Place a "0" in the "4-B" slot.
   ➢ Continue to next "A-Row" number.

4. Can you subtract 2 from 3 = Yes (Which is "1" in binary).
   ➢ Place a "1" in the "2-B" slot.
   ➢ What remains of the original number?
      o 3 – 2 = 1 (In decimal).
      o Now use "1" as the number in the "C" slot.
   ➢ Continue to next "A-Row" number.

5. Can you subtract 1 from 1 = Yes (Which is "1" in binary).
   ➢ Place a "1" in the "1-B" slot.
   ➢ What remains of the original number?
      o 0 (In decimal).

- All bits on the "Left Side" have been created resulting in "0011" which is the "nibble" for the hexadecimal character "3". Below:

	Hex to Binary Conversions							
A	8	4	2	1	8	4	2	1
B	0	0	1	1				
C	Left = 3				Right = C (12)			

- Now continue to do the same for the "Right Side" which has the character "C".

    1. Ask the question "Is this a LETTER or a NUMBER?"
        ➢ If character is a LETTER use conversion chart to change to correlated number and go to step #2.
           ○ The character "C" equals the decimal number "12". Insert "12" into the "C-Right" box and subtract all "B-Row" numbers from "12".

Hex	Represents
A	10
B	11
C	12
D	13
E	14
F	15

        ➢ If character is a NUMBER, continue to step #2.
    2. Can you subtract 8 from 12 = Yes (Which is "1" in binary).
        ➢ Place a "1" in the "8-B" slot.
        ➢ What remains of the original number?
           ○ 12 – 8 = 4 (In decimal).
           ○ Now use "4" as the number in the "C" slot.
        ➢ Continue to next "A-Row" number.
    3. Can you subtract 4 from 4 = Yes (Which is "1" in binary).
        ➢ Place a "1" in the "4-B" slot.
        ➢ What remains of the original number?
           ○ 4 – 4 = 0 (In decimal).
           ○ Now use "0" as the number in the "C" slot.
        ➢ Place a "0" in the "4-B" slot.
        ➢ Continue to next "A-Row" number.
    4. Can you subtract 2 from 0 = No (Which is "0" in binary).
        ➢ Place a "0" in the "2-B" slot.
        ➢ Continue to next "A-Row" number.
    5. Can you subtract 1 from 0 = No (Which is "0" in binary).

- All bits on the "Right Side" have been created resulting in "1100" which is the "nibble" for the hexadecimal character "C". The results appear as follows:

Hex to Binary Conversions

	8	4	2	1	8	4	2	1
A	8	4	2	1	8	4	2	1
B	0	0	1	1	1	1	0	0
C	Left = 3				Right = C (12)			

- This give us the total answer that the hexadecimal combination "3C" = "00111100" in binary! Outstanding!!! Let's try another!

Take the following example: Given the MAC address of 23-3C-DD-AB-FE-72, what is the binary version of the 4th character set? Let's work the problem:
- 4th character set = "AB"
- Place the characters on the conversion chart as in the following (Remember to convert "Letters" into corresponding "Numbers"):

Hex to Binary Conversions

	8	4	2	1	8	4	2	1
A	8	4	2	1	8	4	2	1
B								
C	Left = A (10)				Right = B (11)			

- Begin the subtraction process on the "Left-Side" with the character "A":
  1. Ask the question "Is this a LETTER or a NUMBER?"
     - We can see that the letter "A" has a decimal value of "10". Now continue to step #2.

Hex	Represents
A	10
B	11
C	12
D	13
E	14
F	15

2. Can you subtract 8 from 10 = Yes (Which is "1" in binary).
   - Place a "1" in the "8-B" slot.
   - What remains of the original number?
     - 10 – 8 = 2 (In decimal).
     - Now use "2" as the number in the "C" slot.
   - Continue to next "A-Row" number.
3. Can you subtract 4 from 2 = No (Which is "0" in binary).
   - Place a "0" in the "4-B" slot.
   - Continue to next "A-Row" number.
4. Can you subtract 2 from 2 = Yes (Which is "1" in binary).
   - Place a "1" in the "2-B" slot.
   - What remains of the original number?
     - 2 – 2 = 0 (In decimal).
     - Now use "0" as the number in the "C" slot.
   - Continue to next "A-Row" number.
5. Can you subtract 1 from 0 = No (Which is "1" in binary).
   - Place a "0" in the "1-B" slot.

- All bits on the "Left Side" have been created resulting in "1010" which is the "nibble" for the hexadecimal character "A" as in below:

	Hex to Binary Conversions							
A	8	4	2	1	8	4	2	1
B	1	0	1	0				
C	Left = A (10)				Right = B (11)			

- Now continue to do the same for the "Right Side" which has the character "B".
  1. Ask the question "Is this a LETTER or a NUMBER?"
     - If character is a LETTER use conversion chart to change to correlated number and go to step #2.
       - The character "B" equals the decimal number "11". Insert "11" into the "C-Right" box and subtract all "B-Row" numbers from "11".

Hex	Represents
A	10
B	11
C	12
D	13
E	14
F	15

  2. Can you subtract 8 from 11 = Yes (Which is "1" in binary).
     - Place a "1" in the "8-B" slot.
     - What remains of the original number?
       - 11 – 8 = 3 (In decimal).
       - Now use "3" as the number in the "C" slot.
     - Continue to next "A-Row" number.
  3. Can you subtract 4 from 3 = No (Which is "0" in binary).
     - Place a "0" in the "4-B" slot.
     - Continue to next "A-Row" number.
  4. Can you subtract 2 from 3 = Yes (Which is "1" in binary).
     - Place a "1" in the "2-B" slot.
     - What remains of the original number?
       - 3 – 2 = 1 (In decimal).
       - Now use "1" as the number in the "C" slot.
     - Continue to next "A-Row" number.
  5. Can you subtract 1 from 1 = Yes (Which is "1" in binary).
     - Place a "1" in the "1-B" slot.
     - What remains of the original number?
       - 1 – 1 = 0 (In decimal).

6. All bits on the "Right Side" have been created resulting in "1011" which is the "nibble" for the hexadecimal character "B". The results appear as follows:

Hex to Binary Conversions								
A	8	4	2	1	8	4	2	1
B	1	0	1	0	1	0	1	1
C	Left = A (10)				Right = B (11)			

- This give us the total answer that the hexadecimal combination "AB" = "10101011" in binary! Make up a few of your own and practice!

Because a MAC is unique and does not change, there is no major need to configure them (Unless creating more secure networks using IP version 6). In the field of server technology, however, there are requirements of understanding the construction of a MAC address. Although the hexadecimal characters are in groups of two,..there are actually two major sections of a MAC address. They are identified as the "First Six" and the "Last Six" characters as follows:

- **CC:CC:CC:MM:MM:MM**
- **CC-CC-CC-MM-MM-MM**

  - **First Six Characters (Represented by "CC")** = Represent the company or business which originally created the network interface such as "Dell", "IBM", etc. Each company which manufactures network interfaces are issued this unique number from Arpanet and the Department of Defense for security reasons. The MAC address of a device is often used to track down cyber criminals. All companies which create network interfaces keep records of all of them and where the card was installed or sold. You can insert the first six characters in an internet search and locate which company originally created or sold the network interface.

  - **Last Six Characters (Represented by "MM")** = identify the special make, model or creation date of the network interface. Often times, groups of the characters indicate that the model has special features such as "Wake on LAN" which would allow a computer to be turned on as long as it is connected to a network. Some high-end network interfaces are actually "mini-computers" which allow complete control of an entire computer even when the computer's power state is turned off.

IPv6 Hexadecimal to Binary Conversions:

The following are some examples of how to read and convert the sections of an IPv6 IP address. We will keep it simple by using what is known as a "broadcast IPv6 Address which reads as "FFFF:FFFF:FFFF:FFFF:FFFF:FFFF:FFFF:FFFF". You will notice that there are 8 sections which are separated by colons (:). Each of those section is actually 16 binary "ones (1)". If the same address was displayed in binary, it would look like the following (For ease viewing, the 8 sections are separated into different colors.):

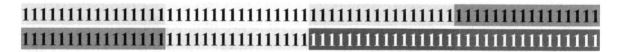

Counting all the bits from left to right, you notice that there are a total of 128-bits. When the bits are converted into hexadecimal, colons separate (:) every 16 bits creating 8 sections called "hextets" or "hexwords" as in "FFFF:FFFF:FFFF:FFFF:FFFF:FFFF:FFFF:FFFF". Each character (Not including the colons) represent the value of 4 binary characters. In the example we are using, each "F" is actually 4 binary "ones", as hexadecimal "F" = Binary "1111" and "Hexadecimal "FF" = binary "11111111". Let's take the explanation even further with the following examples:

- Hex FFFF = Binary of 1111111111111111
- Hex 0000 = Binary of 0000000000000000
- Hex D4DB = Binary of 1101010011011011

Ipv6 Address Concepts and Sections.

Ipv6 Address Concepts and Sections:

When using IPv6 it is required to understand the different sections included in the 128-bit identity. Similar to IPv4 sections which include a network section/ID, host section/ID and netmask indicator, IPv6 addresses have sections which provide similar functions but use different names. The following are the sections for IPv6:

- **Prefix** = Often times, internet service providers supply available IPv6 public addresses with the first 64 bits representing the entire network (Often indicated by "/64" appearing after the IP address). This requires every system on that network to have an identical collection of bits moving from the "Left-to-Right".
  - o Utilizes the bits moving from "Left-to-Right" (Often called the "Leftmost Bits").
  - o Devices on the same network will have a matching arrangement of "0's" and "1's" on the leftmost side.
  - o Expressed with a "/" similar to CIDR.
  - o Comparable to an IPv4 subnet mask.
  - o Examples of 4 systems in the same network would be as follows:
    - ➤ 2001:0db8:fd30:7654:1085:0099:fecc:5871 /64
    - ➤ 2001:0db8: fd30:7654:abcd:0052:e433:0001 /64
    - ➤ 2001:0db8: fd30:7654:dea0:8766:d222:98cc /64
    - ➤ 2001:0db8: fd30:7654:76ff:0433:5432:bb98 /64
      - ☐ The "/64" indicates that 1st 64 bits moving from "left-to-right" on all the nodes are identical.

- **Interface ID** = On a flat network, this will be the last 64bits of the IP address after the Prefix section. This section is used for the unique identifier of the specific node. Below, the section highlighted in "BOLD BLACK" would represent the interface ID. Examples of 4 systems in the same network would be as follows:
  - o 2001:0db8:fd30:7654:1085:0099:fecc:5871 /64
  - o 2001:0db8:fd30:7654:abcd:0052:e433:0001 /64
  - o 2001:0db8:fd30:7654:dea0:8766:d222:98cc /64
  - o 2001:0db8:fd30:7654:76ff:0433:5432:bb98 /64

IP v6 written format methods:

Preferred Format = IPv6 addresses are very long in written format. This is what is called the "Preferred Format" which requires the display of all 32 hexadecimal characters. Below are examples of this format:

- 2001:0db8:0000:0000:0000:0578:abcd:00cb
- 2001:0000:abcd:0cbd:0000:321c:951d:fe35
- Fe80:1700:0000:00ce:0000:0000:0000:567d

Compressed Format = There are two options however which can be used to reduce the written/displayed characters of the IP address although all 128 bits are still being utilized. This method is referred to as "Compressed Format". The two methods are as follows:

- **Method #1** = Any leading hexadecimal 0's (zero's) in any 16-bit section (hextet) can be omitted:
- **Method #2** = Any string of one or more hexadecimal 0's (zero's) in a complete 16-bit segments (hextets) can be replace with a zero (0) between colons or simply a double colon (::).
  - o The double colon (::) can only be used once within an address.
  - o This is commonly known as "Compressed Format".

Let's evaluate the method #1 which allows any leading hexadecimal zero's ("0's") in any 16-bit section (hextet) to be omitted. Using a single hextet example, notice how the method can be implemented:

- "01AB" can be written as "1AB"
- "09F0" can be written as "9F0"
- "0A00" can be written as "A00"
- "0000" can be written as ":0:"

Below are full text examples using the leading zero removal method:

Example 1:

- Preferred Format = 2001:0db8:0000:0000:0000:0578:abcd:00cb
- Preceding Zero Removal Format = 2001:db8:0000:0000:0000:578:abcd:cb

Example 1:

- Preferred Format = 2001:0000:00cd:0cbd:0000:021c:951d:0035
- Preceding Zero Removal Format = 2001:0000:cd:cbd:0000:21c:951d:35

Let's evaluate the method #2 which allows any string of one or more 16-bit segments (hextets) consisting of all 0's to be replaced with a zero between colons (:0:) or simply a double colon (::).

- Note: The double colon (::) can only be used once within an address.
- This is commonly known as "Compressed Format".
- Using a four hextet example, notice how the method can be implemented:
  - "**FE80:0000:0000:CD00**" can be written as "**FE80::CD00**"
  - "**FE80:1234:0000:0000**" can be written as "**FE80:1234:0:**"
  - "**FE80:0000:0000:0000**" can be written as "**FE80::**"

Below are additional examples using the Compression Method (Note, the syntax ": :" and can only be used once in a given IP address):

- Preferred Format = 2001:0db8:0000:0000:0000:0578:abcd:00cb
  - Compressed Format = 2001:0db8:0:0:0:0578:abcd:00cb
  - Or: 2001:0db8: :0578:abcd:00cb

- Preferred Format = 2001:0000:abcd:0cbd:0000:321c:951d:fe35
  - Compressed Format = 2001: :abcd:0cbd:0:321c:951d:fe35

- Preferred Format = Fe80:1700:0000:00ce:0000:0000:0000:567d
  - Compressed Format = Fe80:1700: :00ce:0:567d

Reserved IPv6 addresses:

In IPv4, a number of IP addresses are classified as "Reserved" or "Special Use". A fast review of the following are examples:
- 169.254.x.y = Automatic Private IP Addressing.
- 127.0.0.1 = Local Host or Loopback Address
- 192.168.1.y = Internal private for testing and home networks.

IPv6 also has versions of IP addresses which provide similar functions although they have different names. Below are some of the special use IP addresses in IPv6. They are also matched with IPv4 types for easy comparison:

- **::/128 (Unspecified address)** = Indicates that the node does not have an IP address at present.
  - Similar to "0.0.0.0" from IPv4.

- **::1/128 (Loopback)** = Used to test the configuration of TCP/IP on the local host.
  - Similar to "127.0.0.1" from IPv4.

- **FC00::/ (Unique local)** = Local addressing within a site or between a limited number of sites.
  - Similar to private IP addresses such as "172.16.x.y" and "192.168.x.y" from IPv4.

- **FE80:: (Link-local)** = Used to communicate with other devices on the same local network. Means that system has assigned itself an IP address
  - Similar to "169.254.x.y" and APIPA from IPv4.

- **2001:: (Global unicast)** = Internet routable addresses accessible on the internet.
  - This is the global unicast network prefix.
  - Similar to a public IPv4 address.
  - Static or dynamic.

- **FF00:(Multicast)** = Equivalent to the IPv4 224.x.x.x Class "D" addresses.

Subnetting Concepts and Methods (Dividing Networks).

Subnetting Concepts and Methods (Dividing Networks):

The process of creating discrete sections inside of a larger network. Essentially, the different sections (Called "Subnets") are configured in a fashion which disallows each section to access the other. There are a number of reasons for this as in the following:

- **Security** = Creating a section of a network which has no access to outside resources which would hinder cyber and internet attacks.
- **Bandwidth Conservation** = Creating sections of networks so if a minor section is overwhelmed with network traffic, other more essential parts of the network will retain their optimal speed.
- **Special Use Devices** = Creating a "DMZ (Demilitarized Zone)" section of the network which contains all external facing and security servers such as firewalls, e-mail server, web filter, etc.

When there are subnets which need to function with other subnets, somewhere on the network there must exist a routing device of some type. Before discussion and attempting labs in subnetting, the following is a brief review about IP types:

- **Classfull IP addressing** = Primary method used on the Internet from 1981 to about early 1990's. Using the Classfull method, address spaces are divided into five address classes of "A, B and C" with two more such as "D" which is for "multicasting" and "E" reserved for military and experimental purposes. Below is an example of Classfull IP addressing:

Traditional Classfull IP Address Standards			
Class	Leading Octet	Subnet Mask	Maximum Hosts
A	0-126	255.0.0.0	16,777,214
B	127 - 191	255.255.0.0	65,534
C	192 - 223	255.255.255.0	254
D	224 - 239	Multicast	NA
E	240 - 247	Military Use	NA
*Note = This displays the maximum "Usable" hosts and not the pure mathematical derivatives.			

- **Classless IP Addressing** = Due to the growth of the internet, there was a need to extend the range of available addressing. IPv6 is a method but the primary restriction to it is that older IPv4 devices could not communicate using IPv6. A solution to the decreasing number of available IPv4 addresses was produced with the implementation of VLSM and CIDR.

- o **Classless Internet Domain Routing (CIDR)** = When networks were developed, traffic was routed based on matching Classes (i.e., "A, "B", "C", etc.) with a specific subnet mask ("255.0.0.0", "255.255.0.0" or "255.255.255.0"). Due to the increase in the number of devices, classfull IP addressing could not support the number of routes on the internet. IPv6 was created, but IPv4 will not understand routing from IPv6. Due to this challenge, programmers began to re-compile server operating systems in a manner which utilizes the "binary" form of numbers as opposed to the traditional method of "decimal" utilization. Because of this enhancement, subnet mask octets can include the following 9 numbers: 0, 128, 192, 224, 240, 248, 252, 254 and 255. With this method, the arrangement of "0's" or "1's" which are the "Binary" version of the decimal numbers dictate the following:
  - ☐ **Number of Networks**
  - ☐ **Number of Hosts**
  - ☐ **Routing Paths**

- o **Variable Length Subnet Masks (VLSM)** = Paralleling the utilization of CIDR, the method of documenting IP configurations has also evolved. Utilizing terms such as "Class A, B or C" or the traditional subnet masks such as "255.0.0.0, 255.255.0.0 and 255.255.255.0" are often replaced with the following class "C" CIDR examples:

Netmask Conversions		
Binary	Octet	CIDR
10000000	128	/25
11000000	192	/26
11100000	224	/27
11110000	240	/28
11111000	248	/29
11111100	252	/30
11111110	254	/31
11111111	255	NA (Or /32)
Assumes 1st three octets of "255.255.255.x"		

o As opposed to using decimal numbers as the subnet mask, the total amount of "binary" 1's" in the subnet mask are added together and a two character decimal number is used to reflect the subnet mask after the IP address and a "/" character (Often called a "forward slash"). Take the following for example:

  ☐ Given CIDR subnet mask = 255.255.255.128
    ➤ Binary format 11111111.11111111.11111111.10000000
    ➤ Count number of binary "1's" = 8+8+8+1 = 25 total.
    ➤ VLSM documentation = /25

Subnetting Process:

In order to pass many Cisco, Microsoft and CompTIA examinations, it will be required to be able to answer questions related to subnetting. All answers must be derived manually. No calculators are allowed. For this reason, it is important that a network technician develop a method for addressing subnet questions which is both accurate and fast. In addition, the method must be able to answer any of SIX different subnetting questions, the answers of which are all directly related. The following are the questions which may be have to be addressed:

- **Network ID** = What section of the IP address range identifies each network?
- **First Available** = What is the first IP address on a specific network which a device can use?
- **Broadcast** = What IP address on the network will be used for devices to announce themselves?
- **Last Available** = What is the last IP address on a specific network which a device can use?
- **Range or ("Hosts")** = How many devices can exist in a section of a network?
- **Networks** = How many networks will be available?

The questions are listed above in an order which might make solving them easier. For network technicians with highly developed skill in math and understanding of mathematical formulas for evaluating "Powers of 2 (i.e., "2^4") will have less to learn, but anyone else may find subnetting challenging. In addition, due to the time limitations of certification examinations, utilizing math processes may require too much time. Due to these reasons, there is a process which uses a "Subnetting Table" which allows swift resolution to the above six subnetting questions. Please review the graphics below which will be discussed and utilized for upcoming labs:

Subnetting Table									
(H-2)	4	8	16	32	64	128	256	512	1024

Netmask Conversions		
Binary	Octet	CIDR
10000000	128	/25
11000000	192	/26
11100000	224	/27
11110000	240	/28
11111000	248	/29
11111100	252	/30
11111110	254	/31
11111111	255	NA (Or /32)

Subnetting: Solving for Hosts:

For our exercises, we will be using subnetting using CIDR standards. Using the "Subnetting Table" only requires basic mathematics and formula (Position) substitution. This means that some numbers are only "Indicators", "Placeholders" or "Symbols" of meaning. The following are two of examples:

- Binary "0's" have the meaning of "Hosts/Nodes/Clients".
- Binary "1's" have the meaning of "Networks/Subnets".

The scale in the subnetting table is used to both identify hosts or subnets by pointing to a particular number which is isolated using the binary characters in the subnet mask. The more information required, the more data will be provided in the original question. In addition, the answer of the question can take on the form of an IP address, a decimal network mask, a CIDR mask (Also called "Slash Notation"), etc. Take the following example:

- You have 13 subnets and a computer with the IP address of 172.16.20.44. What is required to derive a subnet with 22 hosts? Answer 255.255.255.224 (or /27)

Yep. The answer was that easy. I just used one finger on one hand! Really! Before we try a question,..let's look at the process. When processing a problem, it is very important to break the question down into all of its parts. Do not attempt to process the entire question all at once. Below, I have segmented the question. Let's evaluate some of the parts of the question:

- You have 13 subnets and a computer with the IP address of 172.16.20.44. **WHAT IS REQUIRED TO DERIVE A SUBNET WITH 22 HOSTS?** Answer 255.255.255.224 (or /27)

Many of the parts are not needed for the answer. In this situation, only the BLACK UPPERCASE section is required with the question part requiring 22 hosts support. The process continues,…..

In order to create subnet sections, it is required to manipulate the subnet mask. In reality, the question is asking "What subnet mask would allow 22 hosts?" When addressing this question, it is important to know that your answer will not render exactly 22 hosts. In network subnetting, your answer will more than likely arrive at a number "Close to,..but not below" the number you are evaluating.

All the answers are closer to the term "At least and includes ……". We will use the subnetting table which has static numbers in specific blocks which never change. When asked a specific number, you will find the number provided by the scale which includes the number just above and closest to the number specified in the question. This will also be the case later when working with finding a number of networks. Let us continue with the process. Using the scale,..you must locate where the desired number would fall. Using your finger,..you see that the number 22 falls between "16" and "32". In this process, we must locate the number which includes or is just above the number specified in the problem. Here we see that "32" is the only number which includes 22. The number 16 would be too small.

Subnetting Table									
(H-2)	4	8	16	32	64	128	256	512	1024
X	X	X	X	X					

Due to this,..although the specified number was "22" the derived answer will actually allow 32 hosts on each subnet. The number "32" was not requested in the question, however. It is just part of the process to find the final answer. In addition, this is a mathematical answer. It cannot be used by the network engineer. There are a few physical rules which will modify this number again.

On any given network,..there are some "special use" numbers. These numbers are often used to divide or describe networks on documentation. These numbers are recorded and used for reference in a number of different ways,..none of which are network communication. For this reason, they are never actually used on any devices. When solving for hosts, we must subtract "two" from whatever number we drop on to reflect these unused number. Because we dropped on the number "32", we must subtract two (hosts) which gives us a new number of 30. Again, this answer was not requested, but it appears in any case. Let us continue to get the answer we are attempting to derive.

Using the subnet table, we have to count the number of value spaces moving from "left to right (Starting from "H-2")." Until we are under the identified number of "32"

Subnetting Table									
(H-2)	4	8	16	32	64	128	256	512	1024
X	X	X	X	X					
0	0	0	0	0					

As was determined before, we have stopped at the listed number of "32 (Which renders the result of 30)" which is a total of "five" spaces from the left. Remember this number. Now we move to the table which displays "Netmask Conversions" of subnet mask numbers. When we are using the table,..we now substitute binary zero's (0) for the total number of spaces we moved from right-to-left. The subnetting table below displays the process:

Subnetting Table									
(H-2)	4	8	16	32	64	128	256	512	1024
X	X	X	X	X					
0	0	0	0	0					

With this scale, we have to remember the number of spaces we moved from left to right on the previous scale. That number was "five". In one of our legends, it is illustrated that the binary character "0" would be used for the determination of hosts. Using the netmask conversion scale, selected the binary string which has only "five zero's" moving from "right-to-left".

Netmask Conversions		
Binary	Octet	CIDR
10000000	128	/25
11000000	192	/26
11100000	224	/27
11110000	240	/28
11111000	248	/29
11111100	252	/30
11111110	254	/31
11111111	255	NA (Or /32)

When solving for hosts (Or even subnetworks),..the question is primarily asking for the appropriate subnet mask to use.

Associated with the binary string "11100000" is "224" in decimal format. In this scenario, the answer must be offered in a netmask format requiring octets. In the process, we have used a single octet moving from "right-to-left" leaving us three leading octets remaining. If octets are not used in the problem solving, they are assumed to be "255". The final result would be a subnet mask of 255.255.255.224 (Or: "/27" in CIDR) to allow 22 hosts with the potential of up to 30. Let us attempt another "host related" problem:

- You have a network with 13 subnets. If a computer is on the network with the IP address of 172.16.0.0, what is required to make sure that subnet can **SUPPORT 800 HOSTS?**

Notice that a big change is the number of hosts and the displayed IP address. To answer this question, you will do the same process as before but add a step. As in the last problem question, many of the parts are not needed for the answer. In this situation, only the **BOLD UPPERCASE** section is required with the question part requiring supporting 800 hosts. The question is asking "What subnet mask should all the computers on that subnet have to assure there are 800 hosts?" As before, the process continues,…..

We are now looking for a number on the "Subnet Table" which is "At least and includes 800". Using the scale,..you must locate where the desired number (800) would fall. Using your finger,..you see that the number 800 falls between "512" and "1024".

Subnetting Table									
(H-2)	4	8	16	32	64	128	256	512	1024
X	X	X	X	X	X	X	X	X	X

The number 512 would be too little hosts. Due to this,..although the specified number was "800" the derived answer will actually allow 1024 IP's on each subnet. The number "1024" was not requested in the question, however. It is just part of the process to find the final answer. Remember that this a mathematical answer. It cannot be used by the network engineer. Due to the process of network documentation and protocol communication, we have to make allowance for the "Special Use" numbers. Since we are solving for "hosts" we must subtract "2" from the number we are using. Since our located number is "1024", after subtracting "2" we have a final resulting number of 1022 hosts that will be available on the network although only 800 was requested. Again, with subnetting, the goal is not to get the exact number but to locate the number including and just above the number specified in the question. Now that we have a number, we must create the appropriate subnet mask to support our number.

Using the subnetting table, we have to count the number of value spaces moving from the "1024" back down to "H-2".

Subnetting Table									
(H-2)	4	8	16	32	64	128	256	512	1024
X	X	X	X	X	X	X	X	X	X
0	0	0	0	0	0	0	0	0	0

As was determined before, using the listed number of "1024" as a starting point results in moving a total of "10" spaces from right-to-left. Now simply write down the number of spaces using 10 zero's. Special notice here,…you may noticed that the answer we will derive will include more than eight characters.

In this answer,..you will actually use the "last two" octets in the subnet mask. Let's continue,….

Moving from "right-to-left", count up to the number of space moved and place a period (.) after the "eighth" space. The first 8 spaces you moved is the binary form of the "forth" octet. Although not listed,..eight binary zero's equal the decimal "0". You notice you have two binary zero's ("0") remaining. These characters will become the last two binary characters in the third octet. Remember, octets have a total of eight binary characters. If they are not "0's", then they must be "1's". Add six binary "1's" to the left-hand portion of the remaining two zero's which completes the requirements for the third octet. The result is two octets.

Move to the table which displays netmask conversions of subnet mask numbers. With this problem, we will look for the binary match for each octet. Again, the section which has "8" binary zero's converts to "0" in decimal. The octet which has "11111100" converts to "252" in decimal.

Netmask Conversions		
Binary	Octet	CIDR
10000000	128	/25
11000000	192	/26
11100000	224	/27
11110000	240	/28
11111000	248	/29
11111100	252	/30
11111110	254	/31
11111111	255	NA (Or /32)
Assumes 1st three octets of "255.255.255.x"		

The resulting decimal string resulting from conversion would be "252.0" in decimal format. In this scenario, the host must be offered in a netmask format requiring four octets. In the process, we have used two octets moving from "right-to-left" leaving us two leading octets remaining. If octets are not used in the solving the problem, they are assumed to be "255". The final result would be a subnet mask of 255.255.252.0 (Or "/22") to allow the 800 hosts with the potential of up to 1022.

Go ahead and attempt the following problems to practice:
- You have a network with 11 subnets. If a computer is on the network with the IP address of 172.16.22.0, what is required to make sure that subnet can support 80 hosts?
- You have a network with 22 subnets. If a computer is on the network with the IP address of 182.16.22.0, what is required to make sure that subnet can support 14 hosts?
- You have a network with 35 subnets. If a computer is on the network with the IP address of 198.16.22.0, what is required to make sure that subnet can support 258 hosts?

Subnetting: Solving for Subnetworks:

In addition to questions concerning hosts,…subnetting question also include locating numbers of subnets. We can use the same methods which requires a subnet mask to be created. There will be small modifications as in the following:
- There must be IP address information in the question.
- Remember classfull IP addressing in the process.
- We will concentrate on binary "1's" in this process.
- The significant spaces will move from "left-to-right".

Let's walk thru the process of solving for a subnet:

- On a network with a network address of 192.16.25.0, what is required to make sure that SUBNET CAN SUPPORT 10 NETWORKS? Answer = 255.255.255.240 or /28

In this scenario, we need first use the BOLD BLACK area then we will use the UPPERCASE BLACK. We will use the same subnet table used to find hosts. Find the number which includes or is one step greater than "10". You notice the number which must be selected appears between "8" and "16".

Subnetting Table									
(H-2)	4	8	16	32	64	128	256	512	1024
X	X	X	X						

Based on the method, we will use the "16". When solving for subnets, no numbers are subtracted. The process continues by counting the number of spaces from "right-to-left" the "16" is from the far left. It can be noticed that there are 4 spaces which were moved. Now we need to start adding some more processes for subnetting. When solving for networks,..the rules for "Classfull subnetting" must be referenced. Specific rules are which IP address class requires which subnet mask. Refer to the chart below:

Traditional Classfull IP Address Standards			
Class	Leading Octet	Subnet Mask	Maximum Hosts
A	0-126	255.0.0.0	16,777,214
B	127 - 191	255.255.0.0	65,534
C	192 - 223	255.255.255.0	254
D	224 - 239	Multicast	NA
E	240 - 247	Military Use	NA
*Note = This displays the maximum "Usable" hosts and not the pure mathematical derivatives.			

Notice the IP address in the question is "Class B" which would normally have "255.255.0.0" as the subnet mask. Using the method in this text, we associate any octets which has "255" in it to be "Unchangeable". Any subnet octet which has "0" in it can be utilized to create subnetworks. In this case, the "0's" in the last two octets. Refer to the following chart:

Subnetting Process Related to Classfull Addresses:		
Leading Octet	Class	Netmask Creation Sections
0-126	A	255.0.0.0
127 - 191	B	255.255.0.0
192 - 223	C	255.255.255.0

The remainder of problem is addressed in the following manner:
- Traditional IP Address = 192.16.25.0
- Associated Traditional Subnet Mask = 255.255.255.0
- Non-Changing section (First Three Octets)= 255.255.255
- Area for network creation in decimal (Last Octet) = 0

As mentioned earlier, when solving for networks, we will be utilizing the binary "1's" to define our subnets. We will replace the binary "0's" in the octet for creation with binary "1's" moving from "left-to-right" as in the following manner:

- Octet area for subnet creation in binary form = Last Octet of "00000000"
- Total number of spaces moved on subnet table = 4 total.

Subnetting Table									
(H-2)	4	8	16	32	64	128	256	512	1024
X	X	X	X						
1	1	1	1						

- Convert the number of moved spaces into a binary value = 1111
- Add binary "0's" in the creation octet after the last binary "1" to create a full binary octet = 11110000.
- On the netmask conversion table, locate the decimal number associated with the binary octet found:

Netmask Conversions		
Binary	Octet	CIDR
10000000	128	/25
11000000	192	/26
11100000	224	/27
11110000	240	/28
11111000	248	/29
11111100	252	/30
11111110	254	/31
11111111	255	NA (Or /32)
Assumes 1st three octets of "255.255.255.x"		

- Convert the new binary combination to decimal and replace the section for creation in the original subnet mask = 255.255.255.240

Using the combination of 192.16.25.0 network address for all IP's combined with the subnet mask of "255.255.255.240" (Or "/28") allows the support of the requested number networks.

Let's try another:

- On a network with a network address of 199.22.45.0, what is required to make sure that SUBNET CAN SUPPORT 60 NETWORKS? Answer = 255.255.255.252 or /30

We will use the same "Subnet Table" as with other problems. Find the number which includes or is one step greater than "60".

Subnetting Table									
(H-2)	4	8	16	32	64	128	256	512	1024
X	X	X	X	X	X				

You notice the number which must be selected appears between "32" and "64". Based on the method, we will use the "64". When solving for subnets, no number are subtracted. The process continues by counting the number of spaces from "right-to-left" the "64" is from the far left. It can be noticed that there are 6 spaces which were moved. Now we need to start adding some more processes for subnetting. When solving to networks,..the rules for "Classfull subnetting" must be referenced. Specific rules are which IP address class requires which subnet mask. Refer to the chart below:

Traditional Classfull IP Address Standards			
Class	Leading Octet	Subnet Mask	Maximum Hosts
A	0-126	255.0.0.0	16,777,214
B	127 - 191	255.255.0.0	65,534
C	192 - 223	255.255.255.0	254
D	224 - 239	Multicast	NA
E	240 - 247	Military Use	NA
*Note = This displays the maximum "Usable" hosts and not the pure mathematical derivatives.			

Notice the IP address in the question is "Class C" which would normally have "255.255.255.0" as the subnet mask. Using the method in this text, we associate any octets which has "255" in it as "not-to-be-changed". Any octet which has "0" in it can be utilized to create subnetworks. In this case, the "0" is in the last or forth octet. Refer to the following chart:

The remainder of problem is addressed via the following:
- Traditional IP Address = 199.22.45.0

- Associated Traditional Subnet Mask = 255.255.255.0
- Non-Changing section (First Three Octets)= 255.255.255
- Area for network creation in decimal (Last Octet) = 0

As mentioned earlier, when solving for networks, we will be utilizing the binary "1's" to define our subnets. We will replace the binary "0's" in the octet for creation with binary "1's" moving from "left-to-right" as in the following manner:

Subnetting Table									
(H-2)	4	8	16	32	64	128	256	512	1024
X	X	X	X	X	X				
1	1	1	1	1	1				

- Original Creation octet binary form = 00000000
- Total number of spaces moved on Subnet Table = 6 total.
- Convert the number of moved spaces into a binary value = 111111
- Add binary "0's" in the creation octet after the last binary "1" to create a binary octet = 11111100.
- Using the netmask conversion table, find which is most similar to the binary value.

Netmask Conversions		
Binary	Octet	CIDR
10000000	128	/25
11000000	192	/26
11100000	224	/27
11110000	240	/28
11111000	248	/29
11111100	252	/30
11111110	254	/31
11111111	255	NA (Or /32)
Assumes 1st three octets of "255.255.255.x"		

- Convert the new binary combination to decimal and replace the section for creation in the original subnet mask = 255.255.255.252.

Just like with our examples with isolating the number of hosts, often times we will be working with other classes of subnet masks such as a "class B". The same charts and methods apply. Let's look at the same question with an IP address in the question of 179.22.45.0.

Notice the IP address in the question is "Class B" which would normally have "255.255.0.0" as the subnet mask. Using the method in this text, we associate any octets which has "255" in it as "not-to-be-changed". Any octet which has "0" in it can be utilized to create subnetworks. In this case, the "0's" are in the last two, or third and fourth octet. Refer to the following chart:

Subnetting Process Related to Classfull Addresses:		
Leading Octet	Class	Netmask Creation Sections
0-126	A	255.0.0.0
127 - 191	B	255.255.0.0
192 - 223	C	255.255.255.0

The remainder of problem is addressed via the following:
- Traditional IP Address = 179.22.45.0
- Associated Traditional Subnet Mask = 255.255.0.0
- Non-Changing section (First Two Octets)= 255.255
- Area for network creation in decimal (Last Two Octets) = 0.0

As mentioned earlier, when solving for networks, we will be utilizing the binary "1's" to define our subnets. We will replace the binary "0's" in the subnet section for creation with binary "1's" moving from "left-to-right" as in the following manner:

- Original creation octets binary form = 00000000.00000000
- Total number of spaces moved on Subnet Table= 6 total.

Subnetting Table									
(H-2)	4	8	16	32	64	128	256	512	1024
X	X	X	X	X	X				
1	1	1	1	1	1				

- Convert the number of moved spaces into a binary value = 111111

- Replace the "0's" in the creation octets with binary "1's" moving from "left-to-right" = 11111100.00000000
- Locate the modified octets in the Netmask Conversion Table (Remember that eight binary "0's" equal a "decimal" number "8".):

Netmask Conversions		
Binary	Octet	CIDR
10000000	128	/25
11000000	192	/26
11100000	224	/27
11110000	240	/28
11111000	248	/29
11111100	252	/30
11111110	254	/31
11111111	255	NA (Or /32)
Assumes 1st three octets of "255.255.255.x"		

- Convert the new binary combination to decimal and replace the section for creation in the original subnet mask = 255.255.252.0 (Or "/22)

Try some of the following problems:
- On a network with a network address of 129.35.58.0, what is required to make sure that subnet can support 20 networks?
- On a network with a network address of 179.42.65.0, what is required to make sure that subnet can support 80 networks?
- On a network with a network address of 200.2.85.0, what is required to make sure that subnet can support 30 networks?
- On a network with a network address of 114.68.47.0, what is required to make sure that subnet can support 72 networks?
- On a network with a network address of 199.22.45.0, what is required to make sure that subnet can support 55 networks?

Complex Subnetting Questions:

Often times, a question will require you to find two or more of the six possible answers. Take the following, for example. The important elements are highlighted:

- A computer on a network has the IP address of 199.22.45.88, what is required to make sure that subnet can support 29 networks with 6 hosts on each? Answer = 255.255.255.248 or /29

The question above requires all of the processes we used for previous subnetting problems. With this combination subnet calculation, it is recommended that you break the questions into the following sequence of operations abbreviated as H, N, S:
1. H = Hosts
2. N = Networks
3. S = Subnet mask

When solving this type of question, the following questions are the elements needed:
- What would be a possible subnet mask for 6 hosts (closest number would be 8)?
- Would the mask allow 29 networks (Closest number would be 32)?
- Does the traditional mask for the given IP (199.22.45.88) support the developed subnet mask if it was classfull (255.255.255.0)?

Let's work the problem:
- To get 6 hosts:
  1. Use subnet table to move up to "8" which results in a usable total of "6".
  2. Count the spaces up to and including "8" which equals "3 spaces".

Subnetting Table									
(H-2)	4	8	16	32	64	128	256	512	1024
X	X	X							
0	0	0							

  3. The "host indicator" is the binary "0" so 3 spaces results in "000".
  4. Add binary "1's" from the most left binary "0's" resulting in a binary octet of "11111000".
  5. On the netmask conversion table, locate entry with "11111000" from right-to-left which is "248".

Netmask Conversions		
Binary	Octet	CIDR
10000000	128	/25
11000000	192	/26
11100000	224	/27
11110000	240	/28
11111000	248	/29
11111100	252	/30
11111110	254	/31
11111111	255	NA (Or /32)
Assumes 1st three octets of "255.255.255.x"		

- We have found a way to support the hosts, now we make sure the same mask can support the networks. First we remember that binary "1's" are "Network Indicators".
  1. Using the subnet table, find the number just larger than "29" which is the value slot for "32".
  2. We count the number of spaces from the value 32 to "H-2" from "right-to-left".
  3. We notice that we moved a total of "5" value spaces. Now we check to see if the original octet binary number has the same amount of binary "1's" in the octet going from "right-to-left".
  4. Double-check the "netmask conversion" table to assure that the same subnet was found compared to the subnet mask used for create the number of network:

Subnetting Table									
(H-2)	4	8	16	32	64	128	256	512	1024
X	X	X	X	X					
1	1	1	1	1					

  5. We can see that the subnet mask derived in both processes is identical. We can now be assured that the appropriate subnet mask would be "255.255.255.248"

Let's Try another:
- A computer on a network has the IP address of 201.16.33.52, what is required to make sure that subnet can support 6 networks with 30 hosts on each? Answer = 255.255.255.224 or /27

The question above requires all of the processes we used for previous subnetting problems. With this combination subnet calculation, it is recommended that you break the questions into the following sequence of operations abbreviated as H, N, S:

4. H = Hosts
5. N = Networks
6. S = Subnet mask

When solving this type of problem, the following questions are the elements needed:

- What would be a possible subnet mask for 30 hosts (closet number would be 32)?
- What is the mask to allow 6 networks (Closest number would be 8)?
- Does the traditional mask for the given IP (201.16.33.52) support the developed subnet mask if it was classfull (255.255.255.0)?

Let's work the problem:
- To get 30 hosts:
  1. Use subnet table and find to move up to "32" which results in a usable total of "30".
  2. Count the spaces up to and including "32" which equals "5 spaces".
  3. The "host indicator" is the binary "0" so 5 spaces x "0" displays as "00000".

Subnetting Table									
(H-2)	4	8	16	32	64	128	256	512	1024
X	X	X	X	X					
0	0	0	0	0					

4. On Decimal-to-Binary chart locate entry with "00000" from right-to-left which is "224"

Netmask Conversions		
Binary	Octet	CIDR
10000000	128	/25
11000000	192	/26
11100000	224	/27
11110000	240	/28
11111000	248	/29
11111100	252	/30
11111110	254	/31
11111111	255	NA (Or /32)

Assumes 1st three octets of "255.255.255.x"

5. "224" in binary displays three binary "1's" (111).
6. Binary "1's" are "Network Indicators".
7. Using the Subnet Table, moving from left-to-right, a total of three spaces results at a destination of 8, which is appropriate to support 6 networks.

Subnetting Table									
(H-2)	4	8	16	32	64	128	256	512	1024
X	X	X							
1	1	1							

8. With the above process completed, the correct subnet mask would be "255.255.255.224"

The process of finding hosts or networks will work regardless of which octet changes. Let's try one more problem using a different subnet type:

- A computer on a network has the IP address of 172.16.33.52, what is required to make sure that subnet can support 60 networks with 1000 hosts on each?   Answer = 255.255.252.0 or /22

Pay special attention to the 1st octet. The number "172" would place the network into a "Class B" subnet which normally display as "255.255.0.0".

Traditional Classfull IP Address Standards			
Class	Leading Octet	Subnet Mask	Maximum Hosts
A	0-126	255.0.0.0	16,777,214
B	127 - 191	255.255.0.0	65,534
C	192 - 223	255.255.255.0	254
D	224 - 239	Multicast	NA
E	240 - 247	Military Use	NA
*Note = This displays the maximum "Usable" hosts and not the pure mathematical derivatives.			

In this case,..anything which is "255" in the netmask will not be changed. This leaves the last two octets "0.0" to be open for host and network separation.

Subnetting Process Related to Classfull Addresses:		
Leading Octet	Class	Netmask Creation Sections
0-126	A	255.0.0.0
127 - 191	B	255.255.0.0
192 - 223	C	255.255.255.0

Also pay special attention to the number of hosts requested. It requires "1000" hosts. The highest number of host possible from any single octet is "254". Because this problem requires more hosts,..it will be necessary to use binary spaces from more than one octet. Essentially,...we begin to use bits from the octet furthest right and work our way to the left. When you start these types of problems, ignore the periods "." Between the octets. We will re-add them later.

The question above requires all of the processes we used for previous subnetting problems. With this combination subnet calculation, it is recommended that you break the questions into the following sequence of operations (H,N,S = Hosts, then Networks, then Subnet mask):
- What would be a possible subnet mask for 1000 hosts (closet number would be 1024)?
- What mask allows 60 networks (Closest number would be 64)?
- Does the traditional mask for the given IP (172.16.33.52) support the developed subnet mask if it was classfull (255.255.0.0)?

Let's work the problem:
- To get 1000 hosts:

1. Use Subnet table to move up to "1024" which results in a usable total of "1022" usable hosts which supports the desired number of 1000 hosts.
2. Count the spaces up to and including "1024" which equals "10 spaces".
3. Write out 10 zero's from right-to left.

Subnetting Table									
(H-2)	4	8	16	32	64	128	256	512	1024
X	X	X	X	X	X	X	X	X	X
0	0	0	0	0	0	0	0	0	0

4. Count the zero's from right-to-left and place a period "." to the left of the eighth zero. This should give you a result which looks like "00.00000"
5. Add enough binary "1's" to the left of the zero's closet to the period "." to render a total of eight binary characters "11111100". This will leave the total binary display as the follows "11111100.00000000"
6. Although the Netmask Conversion table does not display it, remember "00000000" from right-to-left equals a decimal zero ("0")
7. On the Netmask Conversion table, locate the entry with "11111100" from right-to-left which is "252".

Netmask Conversions		
Binary	Octet	CIDR
10000000	128	/25
11000000	192	/26
11100000	224	/27
11110000	240	/28
11111000	248	/29
11111100	252	/30
11111110	254	/31
11111111	255	NA (Or /32)
Assumes 1st three octets of "255.255.255.x"		

8. This binary string of character will be converted to decimal format as in "252.0".
9. The "252.0" is to be added to the classfull netmask of "255.255" which results in "255.255.252.0".

10. The "host indicators" are the binary "0", so 10 spaces x "0" displays as "0000000000".
11. Binary "1's" after the classfull netmask are "Network Indicators".
12. There are a total of six binary "1's" after the classfull netmask (11111100).
13. Using the Subnet Table, moving from left-to-right a total of six spaces results at a destination of 64, which is appropriate to support 64 networks.
14. With the above process completed, the correct subnet mask would be "255.255.252.0"

Early in this chapter, we discussed the idea that there were a number of questions which involves subnetting. In review, the following are the questions which may be have to be addressed:

- **Network ID** = What section of the IP address range identifies each network?
- **First Available** = What is the first IP address on a specific network which a device can use?
- **Broadcast** = What IP address on the network will be used for devices to announce themselves?
- **Last Available** = What is the last IP address on a specific network which a device can use?
- **Hosts** = How many devices can exist in a section of a network?
- **Networks** = How many networks will be available?

Working with the earlier subnetting questions, we address the last two items but we still must be able to derive the following:

- **Network ID** = What section of the IP address range identifies each network?
- **First Available** = What is the first IP address on a specific network which a device can use?
- **Broadcast** = What IP address on the network will be used for devices to announce themselves?
- **Last Available** = What is the last IP address on a specific network which a device can use?

The process for solving the subnetting question below will require the use of the subnetting table of the method chart as below:

Subnetting Table									
(H-2)	4	8	16	32	64	128	256	512	1024

The primary section you will use will be the octet which allows the creation of the subnets. This section is often derived from a previous question or may actually appear in the text of the questions. Using a previous problem for example:

- A computer on a network has the IP address of 201.16.33.52, what is required to make sure that subnet can support 6 networks with 30 hosts on each? Answer = 255.255.255.224 or /27

We will not process the entire problem, we just needed to get the answer which can be written as "255.255.255.224" or "/27". The section we will need to answer the remaining four questions will be the octet which allows the creation of the subnets. In this scenario, we will use the last octet which is "224".

To begin the process, we will use the number 256 as our base subnet number. This is due to using pure math and the powers of "2", this is the highest number for any given octet. After we find out the value of the octet used to isolate hosts or networks,..we will subtract that number from "256" which will provide us our answers. Take the following for example:

- Base number for subnet ranges = 256
- Derived/Given Subnet number = -224
- Resulting number from subtraction = 32

- The "32" instantly gives us two answers which are identical:
   - Total number of hosts possible on each network = 32 hosts
   - 2nd network ID = 32

The following are the examples of all the networks. Begin with the real starting 4th octet of "0" and the subsequent networks will follow in groups of "32 as in the following:
- First Network = 201.16.33.0
- Second Network = 201.16.33.32
- Third Network = 201.16.33.64

- Forth Network = 201.16.33.96
- Fifth Network = 201.16.33.128
- Sixth Network = 201.16.33.160
- Seventh Network = 201.16.33.192
- Eight Network = 201.16.33.224
- END

When subnetting for range,..when you find a host address which matches your netmask, you have arrived at the end of your network. Using the numbers we derived from the base number subtraction, we can get the following answers. Using the first subnet, let's answer the following questions:

- Network ID = What section of the IP address range identifies each network?
  - Answer = This is the number we have developed from subtracting the netmask number (224) from the base number (256) which give us "32". The Subnet ID is the last octet due to subtracting the derived subnet mask octet as in the following sections highlighted in BOLD BLACK:
    - First network starts = 201.16.33.0
    - Second network starts = 201.16.33.32
    - Third network starts = 201.16.33.64
    - Forth network starts = 201.16.33.96
    - Fifth network starts = 201.16.33.128
    - Sixth network starts = 201.16.33.160
    - Seventh network starts = 201.16.33.192
    - Eighth network starts = 201.16.33.224 (Stop here!)
  - Each network has a specific range of IP addresses. Different subnets cannot communicate with others unless there exists a server which connects the different networks. Within each network, there are names associated with specific IP addresses such as:
    - First Available = What is the first IP address on a specific network which a device can use?
    - Broadcast = What IP address on the network will be used for devices to announce themselves?
    - Last Available = What is the last IP address on a specific network which a device can use?
  - Let us evaluate the 3rd subnet which begins as 201.16.33.34:

- First Available = After using the subnetting process, we found that the third network begins with the network ID of 201.16.33.64. Whichever IP represents the network ID is never used. It is used for labeling and references purposes on documents. This results in the first IP address which can be placed on a device to be whichever IP appears after the Network ID. We refer to this as the "First Available". In this scenario, the first usable IP would be "201.16.33.65".
- Broadcast Address = This would be the address which appears just before the next network. In this scenario, the next, or forth network, would start with the IP address of "201.16.33.96". The address just before the forth network ID would be "201.16.33.95" which makes it the broadcast for the third network. As stated earlier,..the broadcast address is not placed on any device but it will automatically be used by all nodes to advertise their existence on that subnet.
- Last Available = Once we have located the broadcast address, we can easily identify the last IP address from that subnet which can be utilized on a host or node. The last available will be just before the broadcast for that particular network. Since our network (The third network of "201.16.33.64) has a broadcast of "201.16.33.95" then the last available would be "201.16.33.94".
  - o Let's evaluate the information for the sixth subnet:
    - Sixth network starts = 201.16.33.160
    - First Available (After Network ID)= 201.16.33.161
    - Broadcast (Before Next network ID) = 201.16.33.191
    - Last Available (Before Broadcast) = 201.16.33.190

Try a few of the exercises below:
- A computer on a network has the IP address of 251.20.55.13, what is required to make sure that subnet can support 12 networks with 20 hosts on each?

- A computer on a network has the IP address of 192.17.101.50, what is required to make sure that subnet can support 4 networks with 20 hosts on each?

- A computer on a network has the IP address of 209.20.55.13, what is required to make sure that subnet can support 24 networks with 20 hosts on each?

- A computer on a network has the IP address of 154.90.85.16, what is required to make sure that subnet can support 60 networks with 100 hosts on each?

Subnetting IPv6 Methods and Exercise:

The process of subnetting for IPv4 is done to more efficiently utilize IP address. Due the design of IPv6, there is really no need to subdivide networks. It is sometimes desirable, however to separate sections of networks for security reasons. Under this type of situation, subnetting can also be done on IPv6 networks. In order to utilize subnetting on IPv6 networks it is necessary to modify the identity sections of the address using the following terms:

IPv6 Sections (Total 128 Bits)		
Global Routing Prefix (48bits)	Subnet ID (16Bits)	Interface Identifier (64Bits)

- **Global Routing Prefix**= Traditionally the first 4 hextets (Total of 64 Bits) on IPv6 networks which are not subnetted. The display below in binary and highlighted in BLACK BOLD displays a site Prefix:
  1111111111111111.1111111111111111.1111111111111111.11111111 11111111.0000000000000000.0000000000000000.0000000000000000. 0000000000000000

When subnetting IPv6 networks, traditionally the third hextet is utilized which reduces the size of the site prefix to the 1st 48bits of the IP address as follows:

- **Site Prefix** = Section of the Global Routing prefix reduced to the 1st 48 bits or 1st three hextets in order to perform subnetting:
  1111111111111111.1111111111111111.1111111111111111.00000000 00000000.0000000000000000.0000000000000000.0000000000000000 .0000000000000000

- **Subnet ID** = The 4th hextet (Total of 16 bits from 49th to the 64th bit):
0000000000000000.0000000000000000.0000000000000000.**11111111 11111111**.0000000000000000.0000000000000000.0000000000000000 .0000000000000000

The remainder of the IPv6 IP address is still classified as the "Host" or "Interface ID" (64th to 128th bit or simply the last four hextets).
0000000000000000.0000000000000000.0000000000000000. 0000000000000000. **1111111111111111. 1111111111111111. 1111111111111111. 1111111111111111**

There are a number of ways to perform the subnetting process. In this text, we will evaluate three as in the following:
- IPv6 Subnet Table.
- Subnet ID.
- Subnetting on a "Nibble".

IPv6 Subnet Table = Using the "IP6 Subnet Section Table" from the Spencer Method we can utilize the same method which was used for subnetting IPv4 networks. The same scale of numbers is used except that the scale has the potential to increase to a total of 16 value areas.

IPv6 Subnet Section Table															
(H-2)	4	8	16	32	64	128	256	512	1024	2048	4096	8192	16384	32768	65536

Each area represents one of the bits in the Subnet ID. Let's look at the following examples:

- A computer has the IP address "2001:3d6c:abcd:0cbd:0000:321c:951d:fe35". What is required to make sure that subnet can support 1000 networks with 60 hosts on each?
    - Answer = 2001:3d6c:abcd:0cbd:FE00:321c:951d:fe35

The question above requires us to use a process similar to IPv4 subnetting, it is recommended that you break the questions into the following sequence of operations (H,N,H = Find Hosts then Networks, then answer in hexadecimal). Let's work the problem:

- Identify the 4th section of the original IP address (Subnet ID – Listed in BOLD BLACK:
  - o 2001:3d6c:abcd:**0cbd**:0000:321c:951d:fe35

To get 60 hosts:
- Use "IPv6 Subnet Table" chart to move up to "64" which results in a usable total of "62".

IPv6 Subnet Section Table															
(H-2)	4	8	16	32	64	128	256	512	1024	2048	4096	8192	16384	32768	65536
X	X	X	X	X	X										

- Count the spaces up to and including "64" which equals "6" spaces".
- Write out six zero's from right-to left resulting in "000000".
  - o The binary "0's" will allow you to have the required amount of hosts.
- Add enough binary "1's" to the left of the last zero on the left to render a total of sixteen binary characters as in "1111111111000000".
  - o The binary "1's" will allow you to have the required amount of subnets.
- Moving from left to right, temporarily insert a "dash (-)" between every "four" bits as in the following "1111-1111-1100-0000".
- Convert each section separated by the dashes into the hexadecimal value:
  - o 1111 = F
  - o 1111 = F
  - o 1100 = C
  - o 0000 = 0

- Replace the subnet IP with the above which provides the answer:
  - o 2001:3d6c:abcd:ffc0:0000:321c:951d:fe35

Let's try another:
- A computer has the IP address "2001:cefd:876c:0cbd:ad7f:321c:951d:fe35". What is required to make sure that subnet can support 45 networks with 900 hosts on each?
  - o Answer = 2001:3d6c:abcd:fc00:0000:321c:951d:fe35

Remember the sequence of operations (H,N,H = Find Hosts then Networks, then answer in hexadecimal). Let's work the problem:

- Identify the 4th section to use for subnetting (Subnet ID – Listed in **BOLD BLACK**):
  - 2001:cefd:876c:**0cbd**:ad7f:321c:951d:fe35"

To get 900 hosts:
- Use "IPv6 Subnet Table" chart to move up to "1024" which results in a usable total of "1022".

IPv6 Subnet Section Table															
(H-2)	4	8	16	32	64	128	256	512	1024	2048	4096	8192	16384	32768	65536
X	X	X	X	X	X	X	X	X	X						

- Count the spaces up to and including "1024" which equals "10" spaces".
- Write out ten zero's from right-to left resulting in "0000000000".
  - The binary "0's" will allow you to have the required amount of hosts.
- Add enough binary "1's" to the left of the last zero on the left to render a total of sixteen binary characters as in "1111110000000000".
  - The binary "1's" will allow you to have the required amount of subnets.
- Moving from left to right, temporarily insert a "dash (-)" between every "four" bits as in the following "1111-1100-0000-0000".
- Convert each section separated by the dashes into the hexadecimal value:
  - 1111 = F
  - 1100 = C
  - 0000 = 0
  - 0000 = 0
- Replace the subnet IP with the above which provides the answer:
  - 2001:3d6c:abcd:fc00:0000:321c:951d:fe35

Subnet Block ID Method = This method is less detailed than the Spencer method. Instead of developing subnets based on specific numbers of nodes and networks,..utilizing the values of the hexadecimal characters, it is possible to simply create differentiated subnets and then place a server between them if inter-network communication is needed. This is done simply by creating an arbitrary Subnet ID and incrementing the hextet by the next higher last character. The following would be an example:

- Assigned network Global Prefix (Compressed Format) = 2001:cefd:876c:0cbd::/32

- o Subnet ID section highlighted in `BOLD BLACK` =
  2001:cefd:876c:`0cbd`::/48

- Subnet ID section modified for networks = 2001:cefd:876c:`0000`::/48
- Creating subnets by increasing the hextet:
  - o 1st network = 2001:cefd:876c:`0001`::/48
  - o 2nd network = 2001:cefd:876c:`0002`::/48
  - o 3rd network = 2001:cefd:876c:`0003`::/48
  - o Continue until you hit the last value for the 4th hextet "FFFF"
    - ❑ 2001:cefd:876c:`FFFF`::/48

Subnetting on a "Nibble" Method = Although traditionally, when subnetting IPv6 the 4th octet is used (Subnet ID), it is actually possible to use any leading section of the last 64 bits as long as enough bits remain at the tail end of the interface ID section to create distinct node identifiers. This method is called "Subnetting on a Nibble". The process allows the creation of subnets by modifying the 5th octet in 4-bit increases. This in turn, changes the netmask indicator (The "/" number at the end of the IPv6 address). Take the following examples:

- Assigned network Global Prefix = 2001:cefd:876c:0cbd:0:0:0:0:/64
  - o Interface ID section highlighted in `GREY` =
    2001:cefd:876c:0cbd:0:0:0:0/64
  - o Hex character used for subnetting in `BLACK BOLD`=
    2001:cefd:876c:0cbd:`0`000:0:0:0/64

- Creating subnets by increasing the 5th hex character (`BOLD BLACK`) moving from right-to-left:
  - o 1st network = 2001:cefd:876c:0cbd:`1`000:0:0:0/68
  - o 2nd network = 2001:cefd:876c:0cbd:`2`000:0:0:0/68
  - o 3rd network = 2001:cefd:876c:0cbd:`3`000:0:0:0/68

As you can see, "Subnetting-on-a-Nibble" is not a method to create a specific number of hosts or subnets, but it does guarantee divisions between sections of a network. As a Server technology professional,..it is up to you to select the best option to address the needs of the organization for which you are employed.

Network Utilities (Software, Commands and Tools).

Network Utilities (Software, Commands and Tools):

Working on networks often requires various tasks such as identification of devices, location of routes of travel and other elements common to communication networks. In our present day of technology, many operating systems and devices include applications and software-based tools to assist in network assessment and troubleshooting. Many of these tools require the familiarization with the use of the "CLI (Command Line Interface)". The following are commands which prove very useful when interacting or repairing servers:

- **Hostname** = This command appears in Microsoft Operating Systems and Cisco Devices. Depending on the platform,..it can display the alpha-numeric identity of a system and/or change the identity of the system. The following are two of the utilizations of the command:
  - Microsoft Server and Client platforms = Displays name of computer.

- **Ipconfig** = Displays basic required network settings on Microsoft platforms. The command also has an optional modification of the command which will show a complete display of communication configurations. In order to use the enhanced features,.. additional words and characters must be appended to the command. The character which must be added is often called a "Forward Slash" or a "switch". The character visually is represented by using "/".
  - Available switches:
    - ➤ All = Displays interfaces, protocols and settings.
    - ➤ Release = Informs the DHCP server the client no longer requires an IP address.
    - ➤ Renew = Requests an IP address from a DHCP server.

- **Ping** = Assesses the ability of one server to contact another network device. Often used to assess if a computer can reach a printer or someplace on the internet. Much like other command line utilities, there are options available to manipulate the data reported by the "ping" command such as the following switches:
  - –t = Continually attempt to find target IP until "cancel" command is executed (Ctrl+C).
  - –n (Count) = Set number of times to attempt to contact target IP.

- **Pathping** = Displays the path and amount of message (Packet) loss occurring in transmission between a source system and destination system.
- **Tracert** = Displays the active path a node is using to contact another node. Will often display the following information about the nodes included in transit such as:
  - IP address
  - Fully Qualified Hostname
  - Time of transmission
- **Route print** = Used to display paths a node can used to pass traffic to various sections on a network. Primary syntax used on Microsoft Command Line applications.

Universal Naming Convention (UNC):

Universal Naming Convention (UNC) is a method for accessing shared resources on a network. Examples of resources could include items such as files, servers, internet sites, printers and many other network devices and locations. The resources are often printers, shared directories (folders) for group access, programs and many other resources. There are multiple access methods available when using a "UNC". Two of the most traditional is in using either the "Address Bar" of an Internet Browser (i.e., Internet Explorer, Firefox, Google Chrome, etc.) or what is often referred to as the "Search Field (Actually, a better name is the "Run Option") on the Start Menu on a computer using the Windows Operating System.

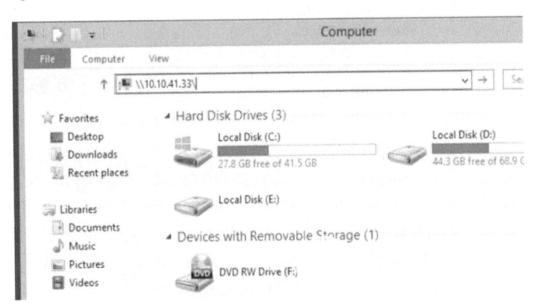

UNC has a specific order of how it must be written. The order consists of at two or three sections which depends on the actual resource of which is being located. The two or three parts would be as follows:

- **Network Device Identity** = This would be either the hostname or IP address of the network device which holds the desired resource.
- **Directory Name** = The section within the device which contains a shared directory or device.
- **Resource name** = Actual name of the file, program or device such as a printer being accessed or initiated.

Each part of the UNC is separated by what is commonly referred to as a "backslash (\ ). The following is the syntax for a UNC:

- **\\DeviceName\DirectoryName\specific-file or Program**

The first two "backslashes (\\ )" command an operating system to "look inside of a network device. The third backslash tells an operating system to "go inside of a storage area". There can be multiple slashes which appear after this point which can mean either "go inside of the area inside of an area" and so on. The final part of the command will follow a backslash and ends with a filename and extension (i.e., ".bat", or ".exe", ".html", etc.) which tells an operating system to display a file or activate a program.

UNC's are normally used in LANs and Domains in order to provide access to frequently used file storage areas. In addition, UNC's often appear in automatic scripts and batch files to remove the necessity of users being required to memorize resource locations. An example of the use of a UNC in a batch file appears below. In this scenario, it is desired that a "Message of the day" file appears on a computer when anyone logs in. The message of the day was created in an application program called "Notepad" and saved in a "public folder" on the workstation so anyone may access the file. The file is called "dailylogin.bat" (The extension ".bat" identifies this file as a batch file). There are two methods which can be used to access the file in the storage area:
- **Option #1** = A user could use a "Search" or "Explorer" option and type the following UNC:
  - \\Unit01\hr\dailylogin.bat

- **Option #2** = A technician could place the file "dailylogin.bat" in the startup folder of the computer. When this occurs,...the batch file would activate without user intervention automatically every time a user logs into the computer.

The 2nd option is the method used more often in the field of computer technology. The following is another brief explanation of the UNC syntax:

- "\\" = Instructs an operating system to access a network device called "Unit04".
- "\" = Instructs an operating system to enter a director called "hr".
- "\filename.ext" = Instructs an operating system to activate a file with the name of "dailylong.bat."

What is a Virtual Private Network (VPN)?

Much commerce is carried out over the internet which is simply a number of multi-connected networks all over the world. In order for traffic to traverse the internet, thousands of network devices owned by individual organizations allow messages other than their own to pass thru their devices. Some of this data is very sensitive and must remain private, but at the same time, the only way to transmit this data is over public networks which creates a situation in which the information could possibly be viewed, altered or deleted. To control for these security issues, VPN processes are implemented. VPN's utilize a multitude of software and devices which allow secure data to travel thru public networks. Think of the message like a subway train which travels inside of a tunnel. The people are like the "data" sitting safely in a metal train car. Each user is unique and gets off of the train at a particular stop in the same condition in which they got on the train. Virtual Private Networks use various methods to protect data. The following are some brief examples of methods for protecting transmitted data:

- **Remote Access Services** = This is software which allows a person to literally view and control a computer system from a location physically removed from the actual computer. A person can be sitting in an office in Texas while controlling a computer in Pennsylvania. The person operating the computer is called a "Remote User". Every activity which can be performed while sitting directly in front of the computer can be done remotely. There are different categories of remote services as in the following:

o **Remote Assistance** = This is often used when a computer user is having difficulty with a program. What often occurs is that the user will contact "Help Desk" or "Tech Support" of some type. Often using an e-mail or a website, the user activates the connection. After the connection is made, the tech can see the screen of the computer user and give instructions on what the user must do to address the need at present. If necessary, the user can grant the technician the right to control the mouse and keyboard as well as record the session.

o **Remote Desktop** = This method is often used when a user is away from their office and requires access to files or programs on that office computer. This level of remote service allows the single user to use the computer as if they are at that location. They have full access to any programs on the computer as well as printers or any other devices locally connected to the computer. With this type of connection, the computer may or may not show that it is being operated remotely.

o **Terminal Application Services** = This method is used by companies, businesses and organizations to streamline computer programs and possibly reduce the cost of applications. Essentially, a single (Or sometimes two servers for redundancy) will have all the programs which are used by a company. All the users in the company have computers but there are no programs on them (This type of computer is often called a "Thin Client"). When the user requires a program, they use their local computer to access the "Terminal Application Server" which offers them the use of the program without installing the software on the computer. Documents created in this manner can be stored either on the server or the local computer. An attractive feature of Terminal Application Services is that when applications or programs have to be updated or changed, the process occurs in one or two locations as opposed to servicing every computer on the network. A disadvantage to this method is often the cost of the server however because it has to be very high powered to support multiple almost simultaneous connections daily.

- **IPSec (Internet Protocol Security)** = This is a method of assuring the source and destination of data. Remember, all data which traverses a network is broken into different types of PDU's (Protocol Data Units). Within a unit, there is normally some indicator of the source of a PDU such as the original devices IP address. Essentially, communication servers can be configured to only accept messages from particular group of sending and receiving IP addresses. Any other PDU's are ignored.

- **Authentication** = With this method, the actual PDU will include a password or username combination to initiate communications between devices. Both the sender and receiver are configured with usernames and passwords which allow a "handshake" proving the identity of one another. After the handshake occurs, the two devices allow the flow of data.

Hackers vs. Crackers.

Hackers vs. Crackers:

There are many conversations in the cyber-security and computer world in reference to the term "Hackers" and also the lesser-known term of "Crackers". Although there is no need to go into intense detail on the similarities and differences in the terms, it is appropriate to them give them mention in a book which examines computer technology. Both terms are attempting to define experts in the computer field who have a great understanding of computer language (Often called "computer code") and computer communication software (Often called "protocols"). Utilizing this knowledge, these computer exports can participate in two distinct activities:

- **"Hacker"** = Identify and exploit areas in which a computer or network system can be damaged or compromised. These persons often work for businesses which create options for computer security or antivirus software. Their goal is to assure the continued operation of a business and to safeguard all data maintained and services provided by the business or company. Computer experts in this area are also often called "White Hats".

- **"Cracker"** = Participate in compromising or damaging computers and other network devices. The term originated from the term "Safe Cracker" (Person who would rob vaults in banks, stores and other businesses). Primarily working as "contractors" or "individual/group" entities, they have the goal of participating in malicious activities concerning computer data, services or operation. In contrast with hackers, they are often referred to as "Black Hats". Examples of malicious activities would include the following:
    - **Stopping or destroying computer data using virus or network attacks (Trojans, phishing, DoS, etc.).**
    - **Accessing and distributing confidential data (Movies, credit card and personal data, etc.)**
    - **Stopping an internet business from being accessed by users (i.e., Netflix, Sony PlayStation, etc.).**

Although, there is a distinction made between "Hackers" and "Crackers", their abilities are the same but their motives define their classification. Depending on the situation and affiliations, they could be the "good guys" or the "bad guys" depending on the perspective and the matter at hand. There are many movies which attempt to display the story of the "person who hacks into a computer system and later gains a really good job in the computer field." Although this is a possibility, remember always that accessing computer data without appropriate authorization and approval may be viewed as a crime punishable by termination or prison time. In the event you are involved accessing computer data for yourself or a company, make sure you are represented by a lawyer. Protect yourself at all times.

Security Methods for Servers, Networks and User Accounts.

Security Methods for Servers, Networks and User Accounts:

Although there is no perfect method of protecting data, computers, server and networks,..there are a number of "best practices". These are methods advocated by computer professionals in areas of cyber-security based upon experiments, trails and even studies of cyber-attacks. This list is not all-inclusive but serve as a starting point for security discussions.

- **Strong Passwords** = A method often utilized in basic level security of a user account or computer is via using an account which combines a "username (Collection of letters which represent a person, i.e., a person named "Bill White" might have a username of "BWhite")" and a password (A combination of keyboard characters known only by a particular user). It was thought at one time that the more characters you have in a password, the more secure it is. After much studies, it was found out that by combining the various characters available on a keyboard actually increases levels of security. Following that philosophy, Microsoft released recommendations for using what is called a "strong password". This type of password includes the following elements.
    - **8 or more characters**
    - **Random letters and numbers (Not in typical order such as "ABC", "123" or "QWE").**
    - **Both Uppercase and Lowercase Letters**
    - **Utilizing symbols when possible (Such as #, *, &, @, etc.).**

- **Firewall (Really Per Server)** = A firewall actually a very generic term. Traditionally, it describes a software or device which monitors access to a computer (Sometimes, it may be part of a DMZ for an entire network). Essentially, the firewall will look for activity which falls outside of a "baseline" (Standard for normal computer activity). When an activity outside of the baseline occurs, the firewall can automatically disconnect the connection or inform a computer user of the activity. As a comparison, think of a computer as a very popular "nightclub" with a dress code requiring a tie for males. At the door of the club, there are staff members who assure all males have ties. If a male attempts to enter without a tie, this would be "outside of the baseline" which will either cause the club staff to reject the male or ask management if the eager club goer should be allowed to enter.

- **Server "Baseline"** = A "Baseline" is a term used to describe the condition of a system based on a history of normal operations. The condition would include amount of e-mail traffic, number of users accessing a network at a particular time, amount of bandwidth being utilized, even number and type of help-desk calls received daily. The baseline is important because it can be used to differentiate between normal activity and abnormal. Software monitoring a network will notice and indicate changes to normal traffic far quicker than users. In fact, if a networks connection to the internet begins to deteriorate, it will be noticed long before the connection totally fails. It is better to catch the failure before the work of users is affected. In this way, the network administrator can attempt to isolate the problem concerning if it is an equipment failure, change because of an upgrade or an actual attack by a malicious user or malware. There are some primary categories of software used to identify baselines as well as isolating problem factors such cyber-related attacks. The following are those categories:

- **DMZ (Often called a "Demilitarized Zone")** = Many companies provide services on the internet in our present day. Some companies such as "Facebook", "Netflix" and many other organizations have computer networks all over the world. Many international companies and banks also participate in various types of trade and commerce on the internet. The only way to access these networks and servers is to have some type of permanent connection with the internet. That "door" to the internet swings both ways, however. Anytime a company allows access to their network for paying customers and remote employees, there is the opportunity for unwelcomed visitors who may attempt to access servers and files located within a network. Due to the potential for network attacks,..companies and businesses often create a "protection area" which exists between the company's primary network and the outside world. In network terms, this protection area is called a "DMZ (Demilitarized zone)". DMZ's primarily protect entire networks. In computer security, a DMZ or demilitarized zone (sometimes referred to as a perimeter network) is a physical or logical subnetwork that contains and exposes an organization's external-facing services to an untrusted network, usually a larger network such as the Internet. The purpose of a DMZ is to add an additional layer of security to an organization's local area network (LAN); an external network node can access only what is exposed in the DMZ, while the rest of the organization's network is firewalled. A DMZ would have a collection of various servers and devices which protect a network from damage or attack from both inside and outside the network. There might be servers which stop unrequested e-mails (Often called "Spam") from entering the inbox of users. Sometime there are special filters on servers which will stop company users from visiting pornographic websites. There are also servers which would stop hidden messages from being sent to other servers from within the network.

Network Designs, Server Categories and General Internet Terms.

Network Designs, Server Categories & General Internet Terms:

Peer-to-Peer = Peer-to-Peer networks are often used in very small businesses. Probably no more than five to ten computers. This category of network allows all devices on a network to be totally independently controlled concerning resources and security. Each client allows users to change passwords, access different files and make changes to programs, applications and other functions. When a different computer requires access to any resource on another server,..the security configurations on the remote client will engage requiring some type of authentication which is not known by the computer requesting access. At that time, the requesting computers user must input the proper security combination which could be a password, numeric token number or some other authentication credentials.

When there are a large number of computers and people using them, however, a peer-to-peer environment can become a large burden for the technology support department of a business or company. Peer-to-Peer offers a high level of security for individual computers but dramatically increase the burden of keeping track of users and passwords. In Peer-to-Peer networks,..each user is responsible for their own passwords and computer. In the event that the user changes or forgets their password, no other user or remote device can access files. In addition, if the user leaves the company or is terminated, a technology recovery specialist would have to be hired to essentially "Hack" the system in order to access any needed files.

Domain = In Windows Server environments, all of the objects (i.e., users, printers, computers, etc.) are identified and referenced in a database called "Active Directory". This database organizes all items which are objects within the network structure. All permissions, rights, abilities, and limitations are associated with an individual item and are separated by boundaries called "Domains". A domain has a primary controlling object classified as a "Domain Controller". This computer, normally using an operating system classified by the name of "Server" is the sole authority of all objects which are part of the domain.

Peer Domain Controller = Networks are often required to constantly operate. In the event that a network fails to respond, it could cost thousands of dollars for an organization due to the time the network is unavailable. To control for the possibility of a domain controller going off-line,..in many network configurations there is the option of creating additional domain controllers which will support network functions in the event that any domain controller fails. These "Peer Domain Controllers" all duplicate functions to support the network. Although all of the domain controllers are classified as "equal", there are differences between them with the greatest being that the first domain controller on the network has all the important services while subsequent peer controllers simply replicate the data. Depending on the network,..the services can also be transferred to other peer controllers if the need were to ever arise.

Proxy Server (Oftentimes, just called a "Proxy") = This is the term used to describe a server which provides a "connection services" to another network or network device. "Proxies" come in many designs. The following are some of the different configurations and their functions:

ByPass Proxy = Often used to circumvent security functions. In some environments, a company, business or organization may configure their network to disallow connections to particular websites. An example might be a High School which might protect against video game or pornography websites. The High School network might have a security feature which protects against the access of forbidden sites. If a student were to know of a "Proxy", the student would connect to the "proxy server" and then the proxy connects to the forbidden websites. Unfortunately, there are thousands of proxies all over the world which are used in this manner. As soon as local government agencies shut them down,..new proxies appear daily.

Caching (Pronounced "Cash-ing") Proxy = Many times a company or business consistently require their employees to use specific websites. If the website has a large number of active files (i.e., captions, videos, hyperlinks, etc.) it can slow down each computer upon access. With a "Caching Proxy", many of those files which appear on the websites can be stored on one of the company's servers. When an employee visits the website, the elements of the website are already stored on local network servers so the website appears on the screen of the computer faster. Areas which constantly change or require input (i.e., "username" and "password" are not stored). This allows faster and more stable access to frequently visited websites.

Logging Proxy = This type of proxy is for investigations. Essentially, this proxy records the actions and internet activity of employees in a company. Everytime a person visits a website, a record is created. The record can be as small as a written line stating the name of the website or can be as advanced as recording every keystroke, photo and message the user inserted on the website.

This data is often used to isolate if a particular user is using computer access in some violation of the company's policies.

Demarc (Also called "Demarcation Point") = This is an area of a network identified to resolve responsibility for service, protection and repair. Every network has one physical connection (Often some type of "port" or "connection" in a wall) which all network communications have to pass thru to get outside of that local network and pass to the organizations ISP (Internet Server Provider). The physical connection essentially has a way to "exit the local network" and to "Enter from the ISP". All parts of this "physical point" which a company can see or touch, inside of the building is the company's responsibility. All items which the ISP connects and configures is their responsibility. The divider for these two discrete areas is that "physical port" or "hole in the wall" called the "Demarc."

Disaster Recovery Methods for Servers.

Disaster Recovery Methods for Servers:

Although it will not occur every day (Hopefully), there is always the possibility of a computer failing. Server failure can have many definitions such as the following:

- Users cannot locate files on the network.
- The websites on internet are no longer accessible.
- Account login no longer works on any computer in the building.
- A computer screen appears "blank" or "black" with a blinking line in the upper-left corner.
- Users cannot find any of their e-mail.

There are thousands of reasons a system could stop operating such as hardware, software conflicts, virus, malicious attacks, and many more. Finding the reason for the failure, is a task for the future, however. The most immediate task is to restore computers or the network to normal functionality. If the employees of a company or business cannot access a network,..they cannot work. Depending on the purpose of the business, money could be lost or functions can be hindered. It is very important that network and business functionally be re-enabled as swiftly as possible. Not only for businesses continuity, but for the network administrator's job security. Understand,..every hour longer it takes to fix the network problem could bring the technician closer and closer to termination. In the end,..it is always regarded as a technician's fault if anything remains damaged, regardless of the cause of the problem. Keeping the before, mentioned in mind, it should always be a priority of the technology specialist (I believe it should be their 1st priority!) to have a method to move a network back to functioning as quickly as possible. If the network is working, less people will overwhelm the technician allowing him space and time to locate and eradicate the cause of the computer, server or network failure. Below are some of the options available which would allow the continued function of the system:

- **The Windows Registry** = This term is in reference to a database within the Windows Operating System. This database contains configuration, settings and preferences for the operating system, hardware and programs. Information included might be date of installation, licenses for access, expiration time for software with expiration periods, etc. On higher order operating systems (Server 2008, 2012, etc.) there are entries which control communications between servers and the internet. Be very careful, when accessing the registry. Modifications are instantaneous. An incorrect registry entry can totally disable a computer.

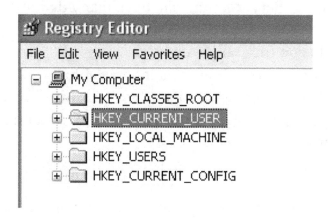

- **Task Manager** = In windows operating systems, the task manager is a utility which allows the monitoring and limited control of processes which a computer performs without user interaction. These process are sometimes referred to as "Services" or "Functions". The ability for a computer to access the internet is a "service", how many times a program utilizes RAM for instructions might be classified as a "function". Using the task manager, it is possible to view how much RAM is being used, how busy the CPU is and how many users are remotely connected to a server. One of the most well-known function of the task manager is the ability to cancel failed applications. In the event a program is "stuck" and stopping the use of other programs,..the offending program can be terminated using the task manager freeing the user to continue to use other programs and the computer in general.

- **Microsoft and Windows Updates** = Due to the speed at which technology changes, there is a need to make changes in operating systems. In addition, often times, after an operating system is released, there is the potential for security flaws or conflicts between different files in an operating system. To control for failures to users, business and companies, Microsoft employs server systems throughout the world which contain corrections, additions and modifications to their operating systems. It is possible to request these modifications be e-mailed (Or even mailed as CD/DVD's using the US Mail System) but Microsoft implemented a method which is somewhat automated as long as a computer has access to the internet. This process runs as a service called "Microsoft Updates". The service provides modification concerning Security and protections against malware, operating system bugs (features which have performance issues) and enhancements to tasks the operating systems can perform. According to many Microsoft documents, many updates are made available on the second Tuesday of each month (Many technicians referred to this day as "Patch Tuesday") computers will routinely check. If necessary, and computer technician can disable Microsoft updates and instead utilize "Windows Update". This is done by manually configuring a computer to access the Microsoft Update servers at a specific time to download a large file which will include Updates (Modifications to the Operating System), Patch's (Group of files used to repair a feature) or "Fixes (Repairs small file errors in operating system)."

- **Backup** = Process of making duplicates of files, programs and even completely functioning servers (Often called an "image"). It is important that these Backups are created at different times of the year (Such as "Monthly", "Once a Week", and "Once a Day") to reflect files which change often. These files are often compressed making them extremely small which allows them to be stored on flash drives, DVD's and even other computers. In the event the original files disappear or a client or server fails for only software causes,...the backup can be used to replace the failed system and operations can continue. All files and functions will operate as if there had been no failure. The "replaced-original" servers or files will not include any changes which were made after the most recent backup.

- **Restore** = The process of replacing failed files, programs, clients or servers with fully-functioning versions which were previously created using some type of backup or imaging software. The "restored" systems and files will operate normally allowing users to access files and perform functions which were supported by the original servers and files. In this scenario, there is a possibility that some data loss has occurred, but the loss is limited to a few days, versus a few years. The only missing items will be files which were created after the backup was created or programs installed after the image was created of the servers. These items can be re-installed or recreated.

- **Clustering** = Many businesses and companies providing internet services such as "Netflix", "Hulu", and "Facebook" require dozens of servers on the internet which can respond to customer requests. Each of these servers consistently check between other servers to ensure that data is replicated and there is always availability to requested resources. Although there are dozens of servers, they are all responding as if there is one single "unit" which is processing requests for users. This system of have multiple computers behaving as a single unit is referred to as "Clustering".

- **Failover** = Due to the requirement of multiple servers being available to respond to requests, it is necessary to have a process which allows the assurance of a server being always online. Some environments utilize a method of having a "backup" or "standby" server ready in case the functioning servers were to fail. Some networks require the intervention of a technician to activate the "standby server" when the primary server no longer operates. If the technician is not available, or does not notice the failure, service interruption would continue. To compensate for the time which could pass between noticing primary server failure, many networks utilize a process called "failover" which allows the "Standby" server to constantly check the operation of the "Primary" server. The method used by the standby server is often called a "heartbeat". If the "Standby" server does not hear the "heartbeat" of the "primary" server, it will automatically start serving the requests normally received by the primary server. The "Standby" will normally have a function which will notify a technician that it has replaced the primary server.

What is a RAID (Redundant Array of Independent Disks)?

On modern server systems, oftentimes, the amount of data required for storage actually exceeds the physical storage capability of present-day hard drives. Many companies have emerged over the last ten years with the purpose of data storage services (i.e., iCloud, Carbonite, GoogleDrive, etc.). In addition, many companies provide services such as word processing, video streaming, etc. These services and storage requirements far exceed the capacity of most hard drives. In addition to storage considerations, the data itself must be preserved and protected against the failure of a hard drive. In order to provide remedy for the prior elements, storage technology has evolved to include a method of combining multiple hard drives for increased amount of storage, faster speed access and drive failure compensation. The resulting process is to connect multiple drives and combine their available space while representing the space as if it were a single drive. The term used for combining the drives is called "RAID". Although literally and physically, there may be 2, or 4 or 32 hard drives within a single computer enclosure, the operating system will regard the drives as a single drive. Depending on the configuration of the system,..there are multiple versions of RAID which either stress increase in storage size, storage speed or protection from drive failure. The following are some of the more well-known RAID configurations:

- **RAID 0** = Consists of a term called "striping". With this process, equal parts of all data is equally distributed across a number of physical distinct drives. This configuration can be as small as two drives or as large as 32. Regardless the number of drives, the operating system will report them as a single drive. An advantage to RAID 0 is the speed the data can be written or read to from a disk. The primary disadvantage is that if a single drive were to fail, the entire span of drives will fail.

- **RAID 1** = Uses a process called "mirroring" and can be as small as two hard drives. Essentially, data is written to which ever drive is available at that moment. After the data is saved, the other drive then duplicates the data. This configuration is primarily configured to allow the system to continue operation if either drive loses the ability to operate.

- **RAID 5** = Consists of striping data across physically distinct hard drives with additional data called "Parity." "Parity" is an "error/failure" correction technology which will allow an array of disks to continue to operate although some of the drives have failed. No data is lost during a drive failure and the system will still operate normally. Depending on the size of the array (Smallest number is three individual drives.) a large number of drives can fail and the system will still operate. In addition, after the failed drives are replaced with new drives,..they are restored by the other drives. After the data rebuild,..the new drives will operate as if they have always been part of the RAID.

Example Labs and Configurations.

Example Labs and Configurations:

The following are some practical labs illustrating some methods of configuring servers. All listed labs and exercises were created by using actual functioning computers and servers. Simulation software is also another option for practicing network technology tasks and activities. At the time of this book, there were a number of vendors who supplied simulation software such as "Virtual PC", "Virtual Box" and "Packet Tracer". If simulation software is used,… some commands used on real devices may not work. Be sure to evaluate simulation software's available functions prior to attempting each lab.

Each lab builds on the prior labs so it is essential that they are completed in the order in which they appear. In addition, each lab increases in challenge levels and repeats prior activities in order to teach procedures and commands thru repetition. As the writer of this text,..I would highly recommend completing each lab three times prior to starting the subsequent lab. When performing the lab for the third time, attempt to do so without any notes or instructions.

Creating a File Share on Windows 10 (Non-Domain Client):

With this example, we will totally disable all security to make access easier. When you work on a computer in an office environment, the settings will be more customized. The following list is not all-inclusive and the associated videos are more detailed.

1) Make sure all firewalls are off.

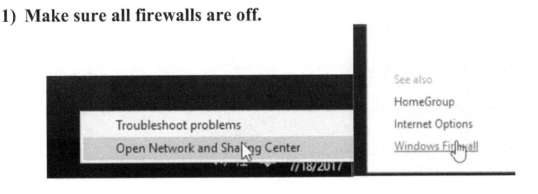

Control Panel Home

Allow an app or feature
through Windows Firewall

 Change notification settings

 Turn Windows Firewall on or
off

Restore defaults

Advanced settings

Troubleshoot my network

Help protect your PC with Windows F

Windows Firewall can help prevent hackers or ma
through the Internet or a network.

 Private networks

Networks at home or work where you know and

Windows Firewall state:

Incoming connections:

Active private networks:

Notification state:

Guest or public networks

Allow an app or feature
through Windows Firewall

 Change notification settings

 Turn Windows Firewall on or
off

 Restore defaults

 Advanced settings

through the Internet or a network.

Private networks

Networks at home or work where yo

Windows Firewall state:

2) Make all the "Green" icons turn "Red".

Customize settings for each type of network

You can modify the firewall settings for each type of network that you use.

Private network settings

○ Turn on Windows Firewall

☐ Block all incoming connections, including those in the list of allowed apps

☑ Notify me when Windows Firewall blocks a new app

○ Turn off Windows Firewall (not recommended)

Public network settings

○ Turn on Windows Firewall

☐ Block all incoming connections, including those in the list of allowed apps

☑ Notify me when Windows Firewall blocks a new app

○ Turn off Windows Firewall (not recommended)

3) Turn off "Password Protection".

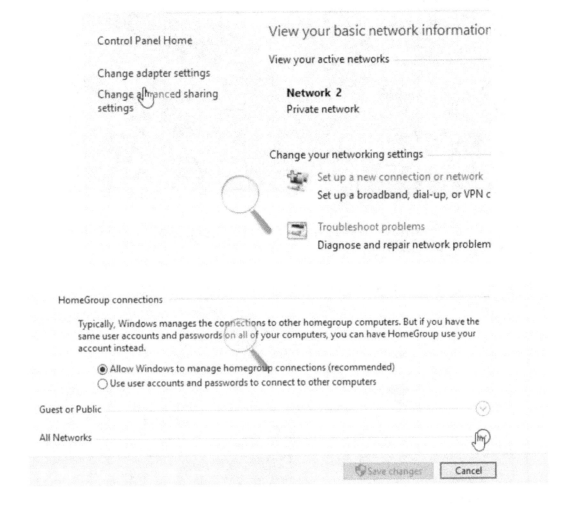

When password protected sharing is on, only people who have a user account and password on this computer can access shared files, printers attached to this computer, and the Public folders. To give other people access, you must turn off password protected sharing.

- ⦿ Turn on password protected sharing
- ◯ Turn off password protected sharing

4) Assure you have the correct IP address and other computers can ping the IP address.

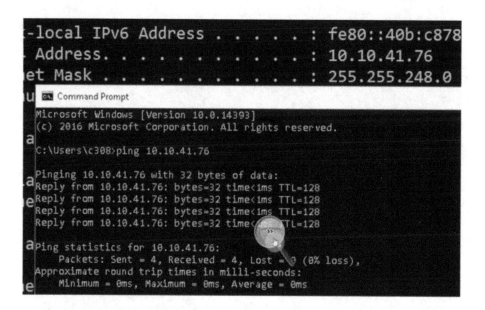

5) Create needed folders inside of "C" drive (Some of these folders are used for other exercise).

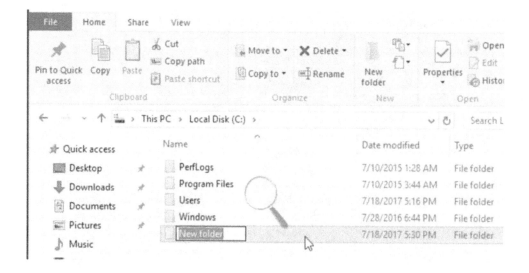

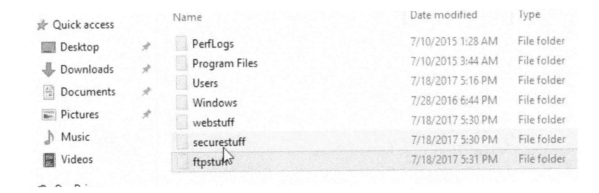

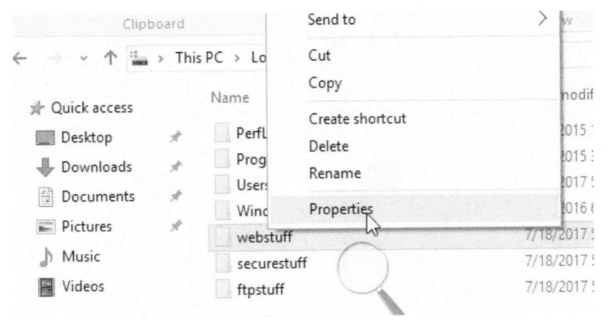

6) Configure "Share" permissions on each folder.

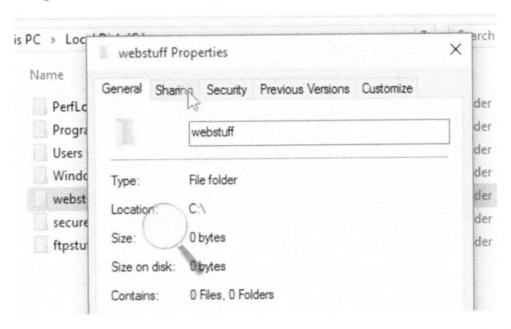

7) Configure "Security" permissions on each folder.

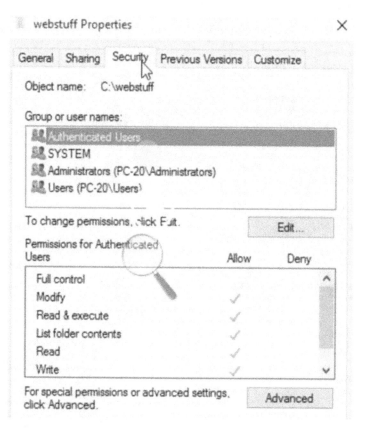

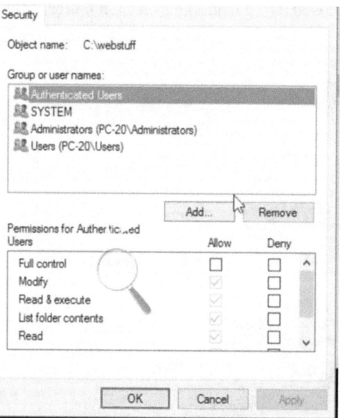

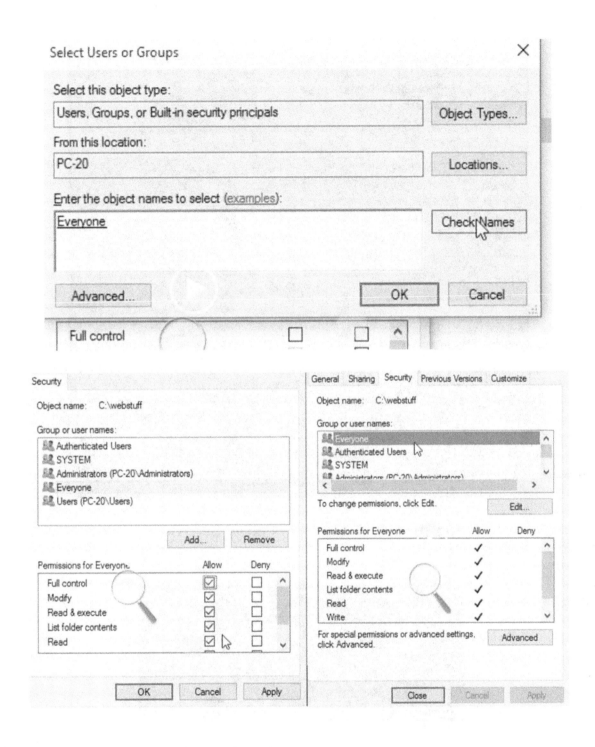

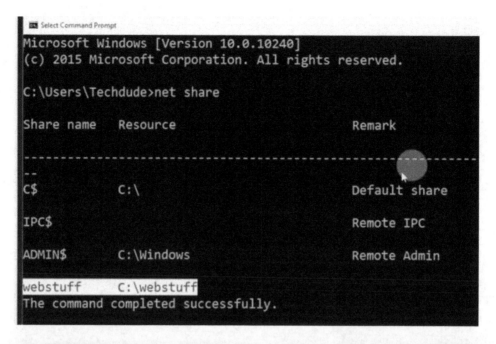

```
Microsoft Windows [Version 10.0.10240]
(c) 2015 Microsoft Corporation. All rights reserved.

C:\Users\Techdude>net share

Share name    Resource                          Remark

-------------------------------------------------------------
--
C$            C:\                               Default share

IPC$                                            Remote IPC

ADMIN$        C:\Windows                        Remote Admin

webstuff      C:\webstuff
The command completed successfully.
```

```
Ethernet adapter Ethernet:

   Connection-specific DNS Suffix  . : ccp.edu
   Link-local IPv6 Address . . . . . : fe80::40b:c878:c
   IPv4 Address. . . . . . . . . . . : 10.10.41.76
   Subnet Mask . . . . . . . . . . . : 255.255.248.0
```

8) **Check to assure that the folders are shared two ways:**
   ➢ **"Net Share" utility:**

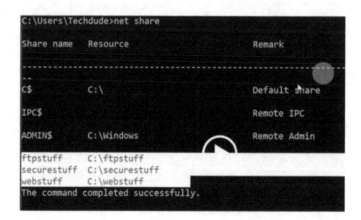

```
C:\Users\Techdude>net share

Share name   Resource                          Remark

-------------------------------------------------------------
--
C$           C:\                               Default share

IPC$                                           Remote IPC

ADMIN$       C:\Windows                        Remote Admin

ftpstuff     C:\ftpstuff
securestuff  C:\securestuff
webstuff     C:\webstuff
The command completed successfully.
```

> **"UNC" method:**

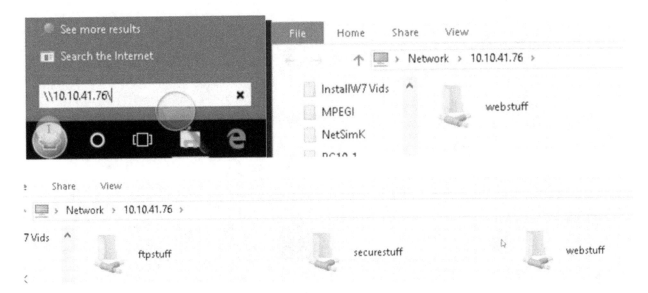

9) **Now anyone on the network who can "ping" your computer will be able to access any files you place in the shared folders.**

Installing Internet Information Services (Windows 10 or Server 2012):

With this example, we will illustrate the process of enabling services on a Windows Operating system to support the function of allowing the computer to be a Web Server or FTP Server. Many other features are available after this installation such as Security Server, E-mail and Streaming Video (None of which will be performed in this textbook, but still important to mention). The following list is not all-inclusive and the associated videos are more detailed.

1) **Access "Control Panel" under "Apps" and "Windows Systems".**

Adjust your computer's settings

View by: Category ▾

 System and Security
Review your computer's status
Save backup copies of your files with File History
Backup and Restore (Windows 7)
Find and fix problems

 Network and Internet
View network status and tasks
Choose homegroup and sharing options

 Hardware and Sound
View devices and printers
Add a device

 Programs
Uninstall a program

 User Accounts
Change account type

 Appearance and Personalization
Change the theme
Adjust screen resolution

 Clock, Language, and Region
Add a language
Change input methods
Change date, time, or number formats

 Ease of Access
Let Windows suggest settings
Optimize visual display

2) Click on "Programs" then "Turn Windows Features on and off".

3) Select the following options under "Internet Information Services:
  - ➢ **FTP Server** (All Services)
  - ➢ **Web Management Tools** (All Services)
  - ➢ **World Wide Web Services** = All services EXCEPT "Application Development Features" and "Windows Authentication" inside of "Security".
  - ➢ **Internet Information Services Hostable Web Core.**

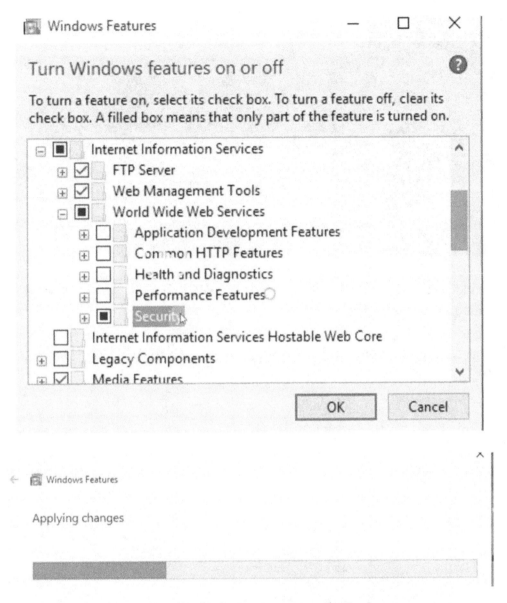

4) **Now access the control MMC for IIS under "Windows Administrative Tools" or search for IIS.**

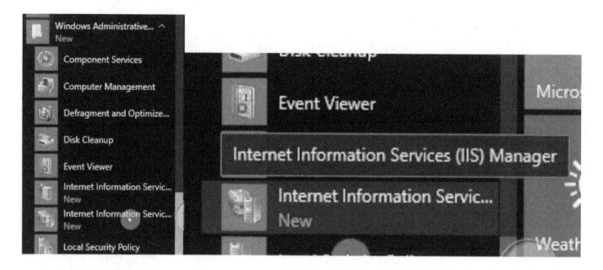

5) Use the IIS vs. 7 MMC (It is the one "WITHOUT A NUMBER" (Microsoft idea! LOL)).

6) Expand the IIS snap-ins until you view options for the "Default Web Site".

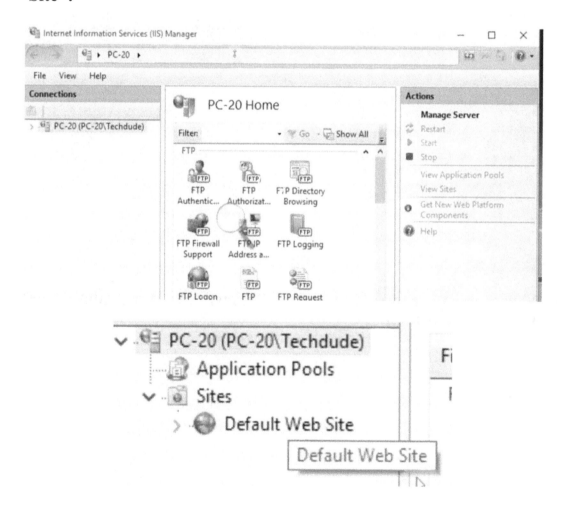

7) **Access the default website from any computer that can "Ping" this computer to see if the default IIS website is viewable.**

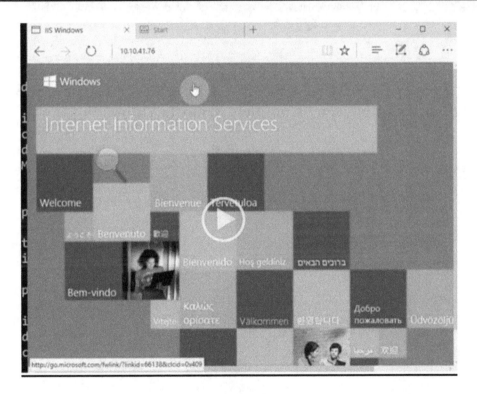

Creating an Open Website (Windows 10 or Server 2012):

In this illustration, we will review the process used to create directories to hold webpage files and assure they can be accessed from other computers (This step done in previous exercises). Assure IIS has been installed on the computer and place a shortcut on the desktop as well (This step done in previous exercises). In addition, please review the associated videos for greater detail.

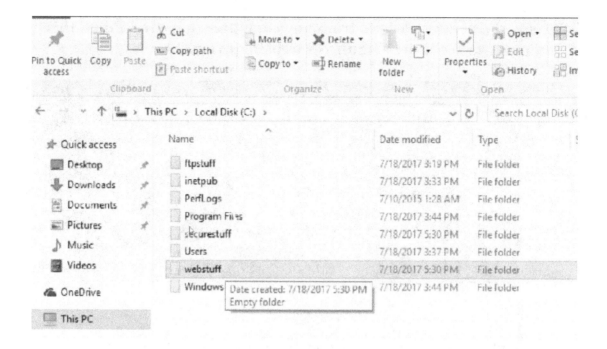

1) Create the open webpage using a word processor and save it with the name "index.htm" as a "Complete Website" in the "opensite" directory.

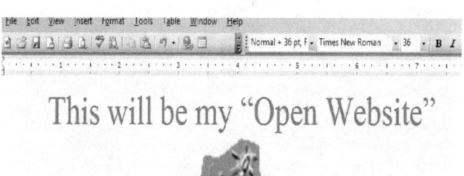

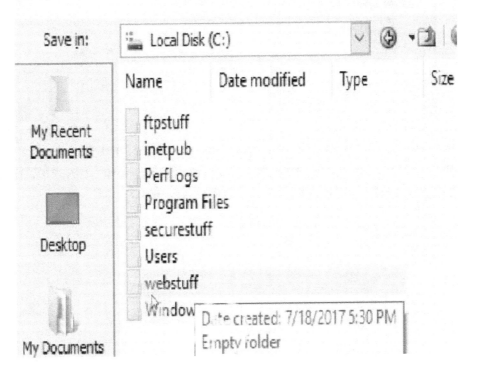

Page title:	This will be my "Open Websi~"
File name:	index
Save as type:	Web Page

Change Title...

Save

Cancel

2) Check the directory and look for the "index file".

3) Configure IIS to make this webpage available from the server.
4) Access the IIS MMC, disable the "Default-Website" by selecting the "default web site", and click the "stop" button.

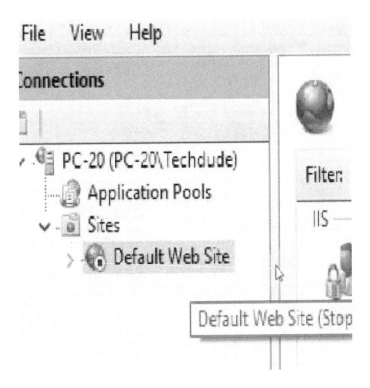

5) **Create the website in IIS by right-clicking the "Sites" snap-in and select "Add Website".**

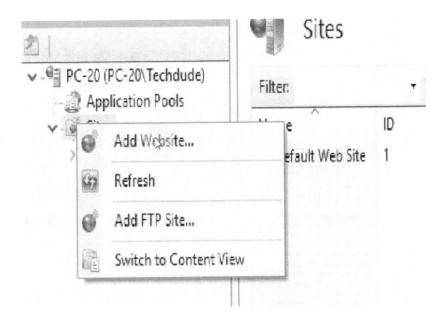

6) **Complete fields with the following information:**
   ➢ Site Name
   ➢ Physical Path (Where web page files exist)
   ➢ Type (Open Website-http)
   ➢ IP address - Select desired IP address if more than one exists.

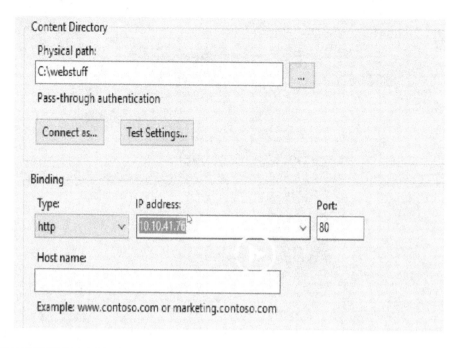

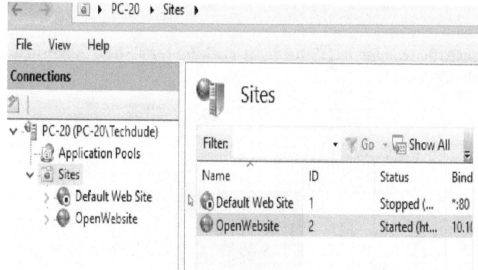

7) **Now test your website using the servers IP address on the server's browser.**

Creating a Secure Website (Windows 10 or Server 2012):

The following will display a process used daily by network administrators and computer technicians. We will illustrate a process to activate and host a Secure Website on either Windows 10 or Server 2012. The following list is not all-inclusive and the associated videos are more detailed.

In order to host a website on a server it is necessary to create a shared directory to hold webpage files and assure they can be accessed from other computers (This step done in a previous exercise). Assure IIS has been installed on the computer and place a shortcut on the desktop as well (This step done in a previous exercise).

1) **Create the secure webpage using a word processor and save it with the name "index.htm" as a "Complete Website" in a shared directory as was done in the "open website" exercise.**
2) **Check the directory and look for the "index file".**
3) **Configure IIS to make this a secure webpage available from the server. Start by opening IIS and click on the name of the server.**

4) Access the IIS MMC, disable the "Default-Website" by selecting the "default web site", and click the "stop" button. Create a "SSL Certificate" for the website by accessing the "Webserver Home" Pane, then locate "Server Certificates" and double-click it.

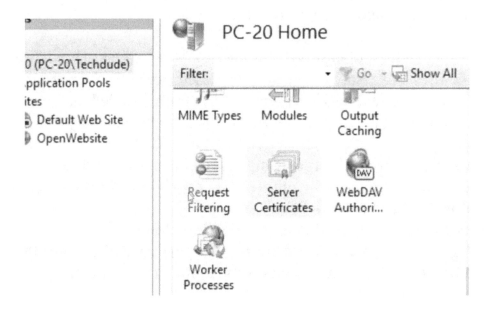

5) Go to the right-side, double-click the "Create Self-Signed Certificate", and give it an easy name.

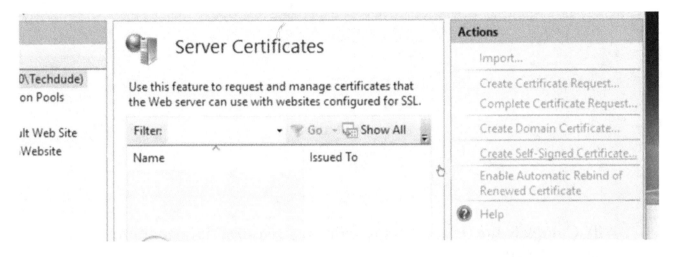

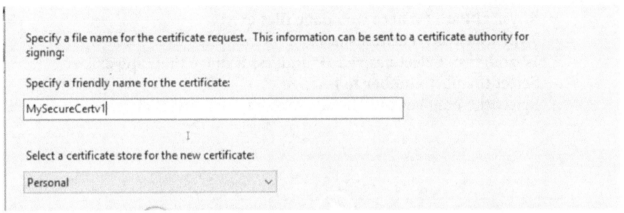

6) Click "OK" and it appears in the list of available certificates.

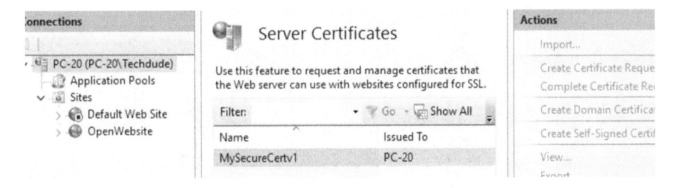

7) Create the website in IIS by taking the mouse and "Right-Click" the "Sites" snap-in and select "Add Website".

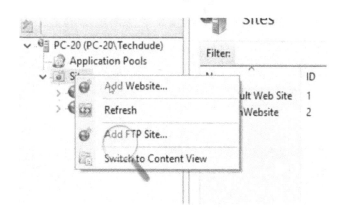

8) **Complete the fields with the following required information:**
9) **Site Name**
   ➢ **Physical Path (Where web page files exist)**
   ➢ **Type (Secure Website-https)**
   ➢ **IP address - Select desired IP address if more than one exists.**
   ➢ **Select the port number to be used.**
   ➢ **Select the name of the certificate to be used and click "OK".**

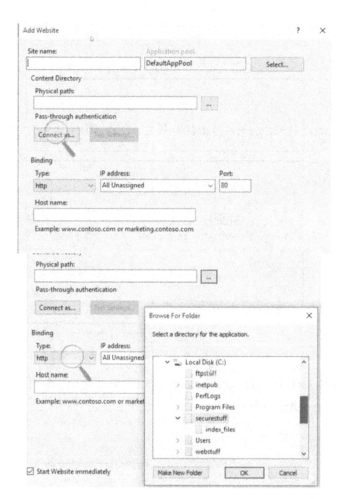

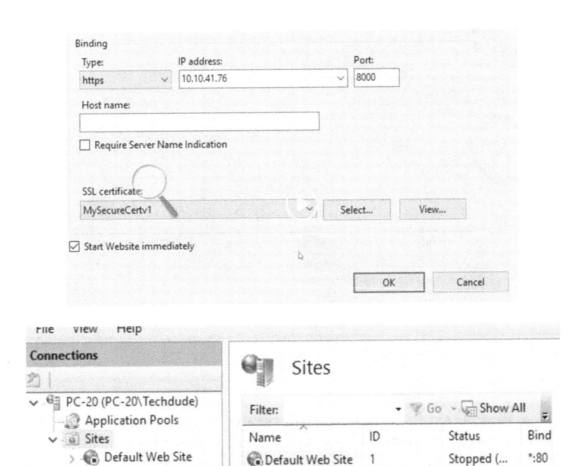

10) Now test your secure website using the "https" and the servers IP address with the websites "Port Number" proceeded by a colon (:) on the server's browser.

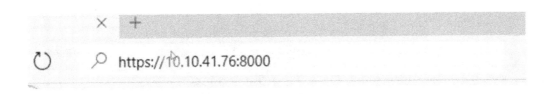

11) Just as before, depending on your browser, you will get a message indicating there is a "certificate Problem".

10.10.41.76:8000

There is a problem with this website's security certificate

We recommend that you close this webpage and do not continue to this website.

The security certificate for this site doesn't match the site's web address and may indicate an attempt to fool you or intercept any data you send to the server.

Go to my homepage instead

Continue to this webpage (not recommended)

12) **This means that the certificate you created is not presently on the browser you are using. This is OK. You can install it later. Look for options that allow you to "Continue to the site anyway".**

13) When the "Secure Site" index page loads, attempt to access the webpage from any other computer that can ping the server.

Creating an FTP Site (Windows 10 or Server 2012):

Assure IIS has been installed on the computer (This step done in a previous exercise). Create a shared directory to store FTP files and assure it can be accessed from other computers (This step done in a previous exercise). The following steps are not all-inclusive. More detailed instructions are displayed in the videos associated with this exercise.

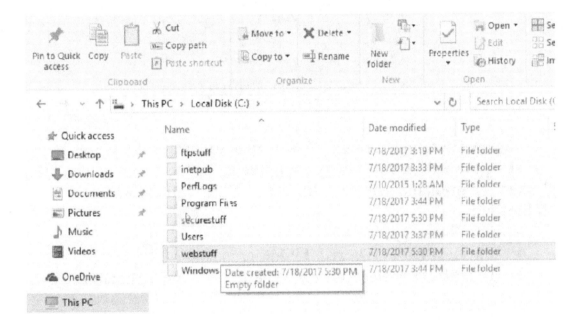

1) Place some random files within the directory that will be used for FTP (Just to test later).

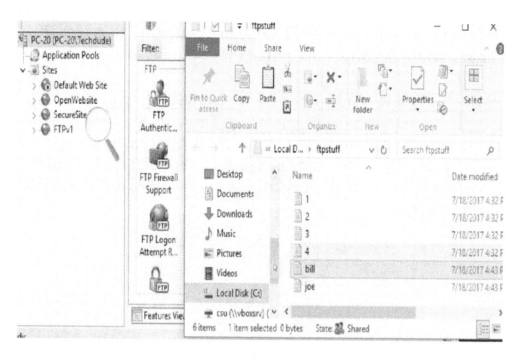

2) **Configure IIS to make this FTP Site available from the server by creating the FTP site in IIS by using the mouse to "Right-Click" the "Sites" snap-in and select "Add FTP site". Complete with the following:**

> ➤ -Site Name
> ➤ -Physical Path (Where FTP folder exists)
> ➤ -IP address - Select desired IP address if more than one exists.

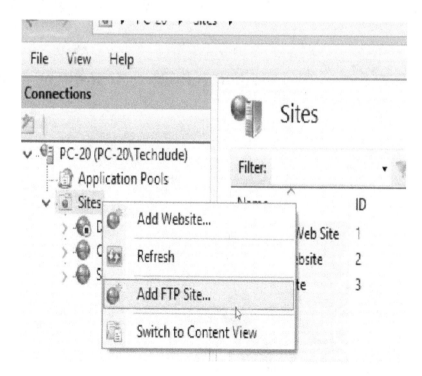

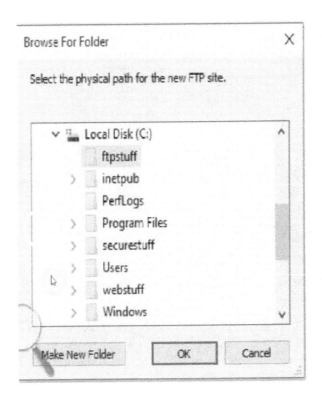

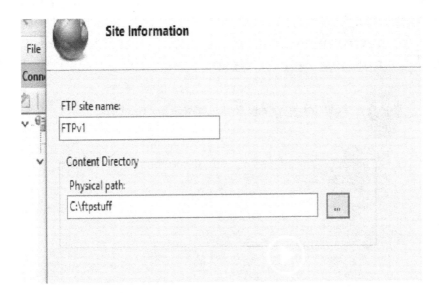

3) **Assure check mark is in "Start FTP site automatically", then select "No SSL" and "Next".**

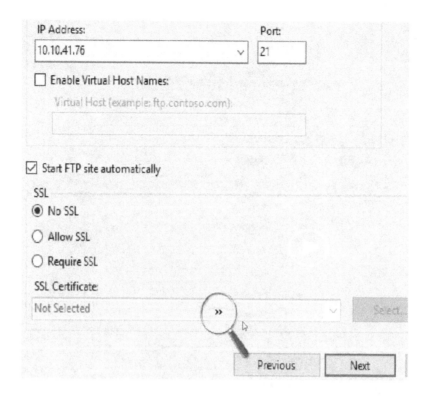

4) Place check marks in both "Anonymous" and "Basic" under "Authentication".
5) Under "Authorization-Allow Access to:" select "All users".
6) Under "Permissions" select "Read" and "Write" then click "Finish".

7) **The new FTP site should now list in IIS. I would suggest restarting all IIS services.**

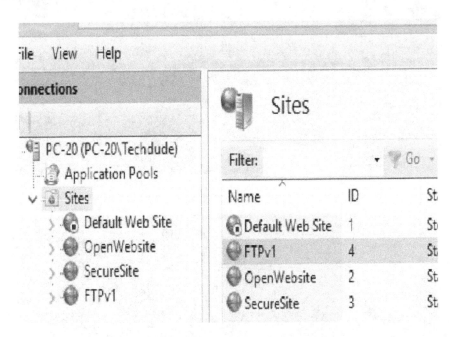

8) **Go to another computer that can "ping" the ftp server and attempt to create directories, rename files, upload files, download files, etc.**

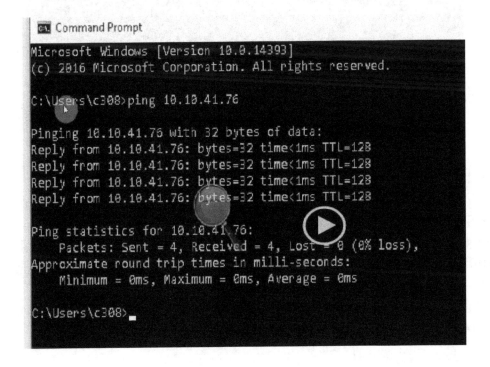

Adding a Printer to a Server or Windows 10 Computer:

*Notes: You must be logged in as "Administrator" to perform the actions required for this task. The following is an example of using a method of adding a printer to a Windows Operating System Computer. The listed steps are not all-inclusive. More detailed instructions are displayed in the videos associated with this exercise.

1) **Locate "Control Panels" using either the "Search Option", "Start Menu" or the "Apps" Snap-in.**

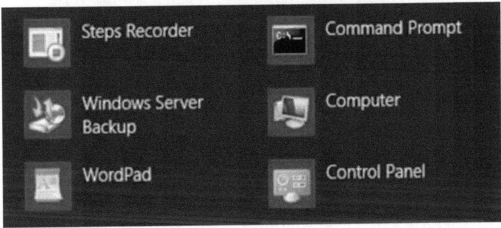

2) Locate "Control Panels" using either the "Search Option", "Start Menu" or the "Apps" Snap-in.

Adjust your computer's settings

System and Security
Review your computer's status
View event logs

Network and Internet
View network status and tasks

Hardware
View devices and printers
Add a device

Programs
Uninstall a program
Turn Windows features on or off

3) Locate "Hardware" which allows the adding of printers.

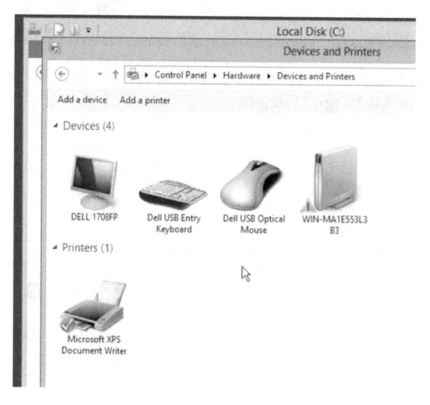

4) Only the default icons are available. Go to the menu bar and select "Add a Printer".

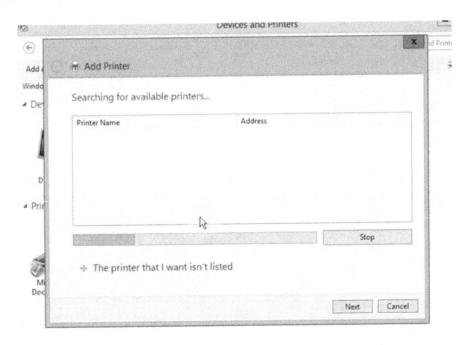

5) A "Printer Searching" wizard will activate. You can click "Stop".

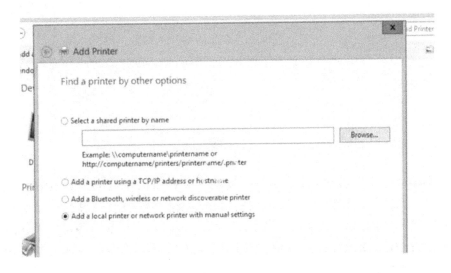

6) Click the Radio button to "Add a Local Printer or Printer with Manual Settings..

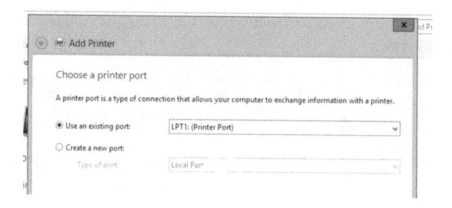

7) Select "Use existing Port" and use "LPT1 (This will work for this exercise).

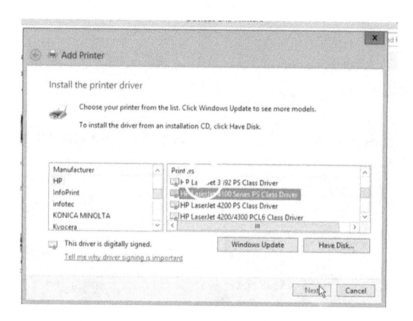

8) The Windows Operating System comes equipped with many basic drivers for a number of printers. Use the "Manufacturer" window and select "HP". Then, in the "Printers" window, select any "LaserJet 4000 Series" printer between 4000 and 4999(Their drivers are the easiest for our exercises.).

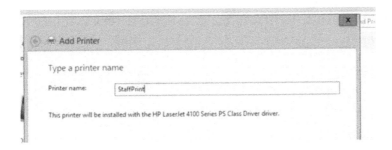

9) We will replace the printers name with the name "StaffPrint".

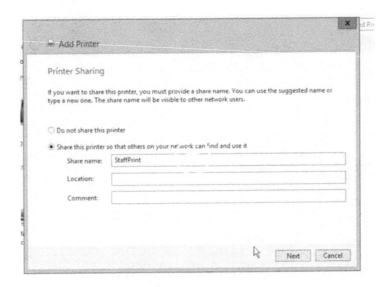

10) We want to allow other network devices to use the printer on the network so it is required to give it a "Share Name". We will use the same name the printer has been given previously.

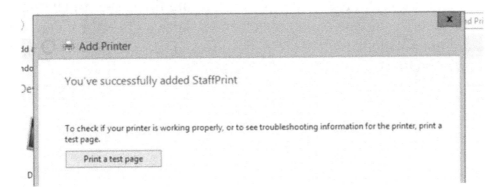

11) **If this was an actual printer, we can send a test page to view our success. For our exercise, it is not needed so just click "Finished".**

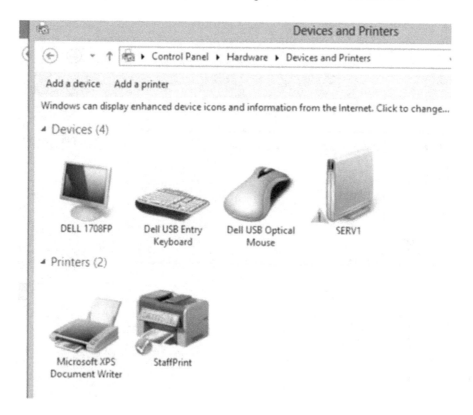

12) **Our new printer now appears under "Hardware", ready to be used.**

Creating a Domain Controller Server 2012:

*Notes: You must be logged in as "Administrator" to perform the actions required for this task. The following is an example of creating the server in charge of all user accounts, security, clients and services on an Active Directory Network. The listed steps are not all-inclusive. More detail instructions are displayed in the videos associated with this exercise.

1) Access "Server Manager" activate Add Roles and Features"

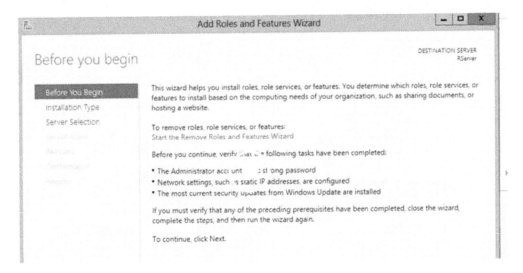

2) The "Add Roles and Features" wizard activates, click "Next":

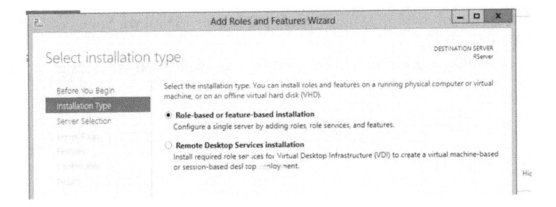

3) Select "Role-Based or Feature-Based":

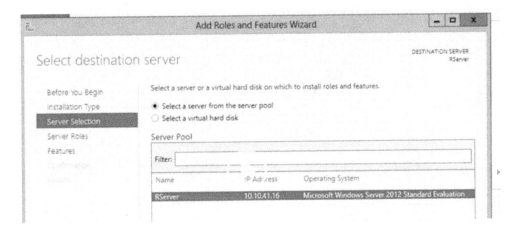

4) Assure your server name and IP address are correct. If not, many errors may occur damaging your installation of the server.

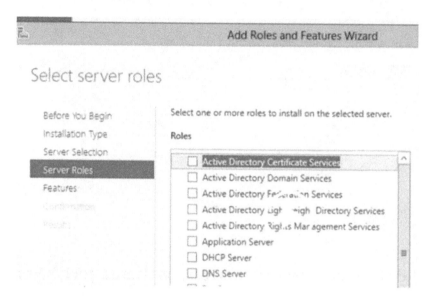

5) Select the following feature "Active Directory Domain Services" and "DNS Server":

   o **Note: Windows will request to add additional services as well. Just click "Accept" when this occurs.**

6) After all services are selected, the display will show "Check Marks" for selections. Click "Next".

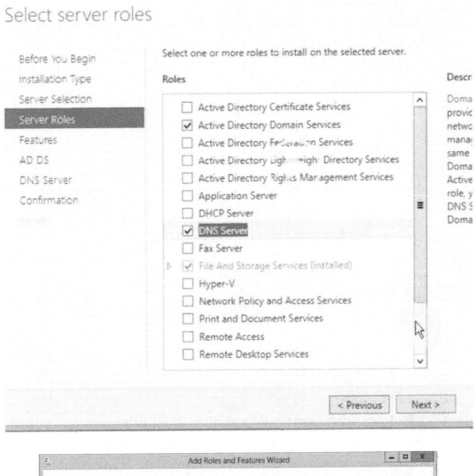

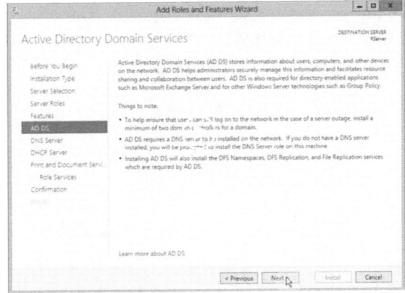

7) **A display of all requested actions will now display prior to allowing the process to continue. Click "Next".**

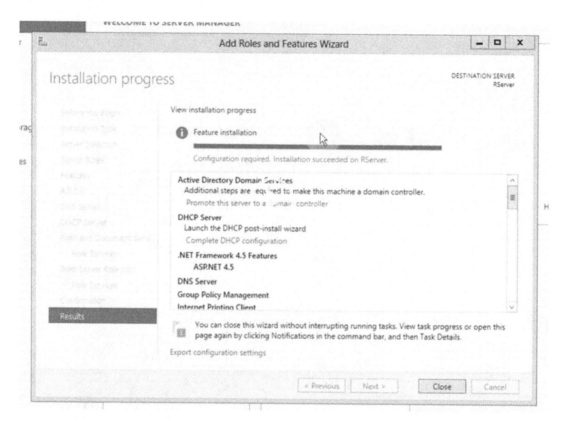

8) **The "Add Roles and Feature Wizard" will now check the computer to see if all the selections are possible on the computer and begin to install portions of the services and software required. This process is only halfway complete. The process continues …..**

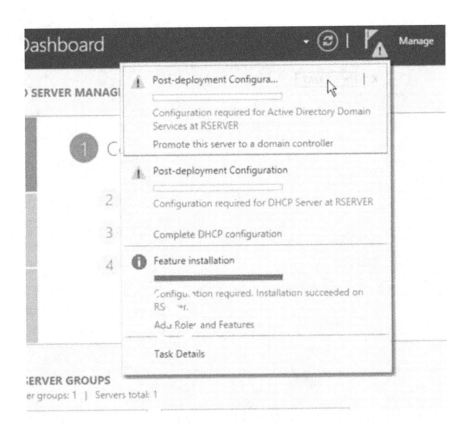

9) **After the wizard completes the first half of installation, there is a need to customize the remainder for supporting internet communications, e-mail and other activities supported by server 2012. These activities are called "Post-Deployment Configurations". In order to continue, you can either select the "Dialogue Box" that automatically appears after the wizard or you can click on the "Yellow Exclamation Triangle" which will appear in the upper right corner of "Server Manager".**

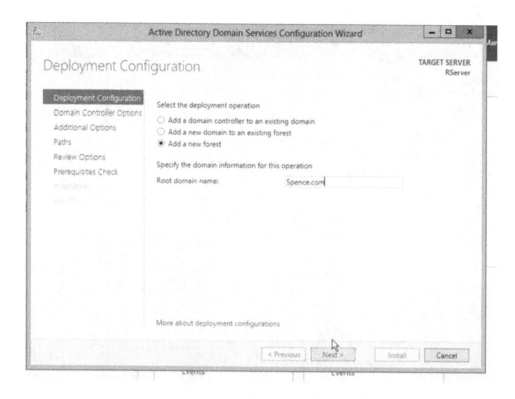

10) **We now begin to customize the Active Domain and controller replication settings. Complete the following sections as illustrated. This will be the 1st domain controller so we must select "Add a New Forest" and give it a domain name.**

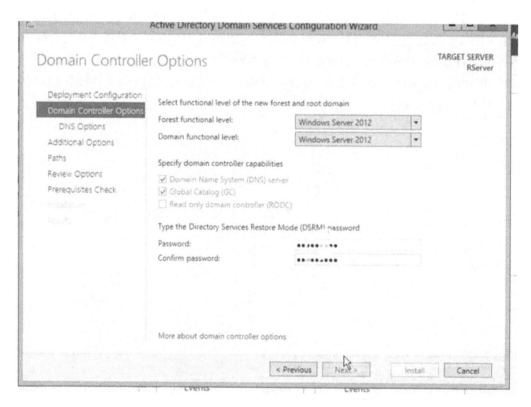

11) In the event the GUI fails, we can do a special restore process using a CLI which would require a password as well. Enter it and click next.

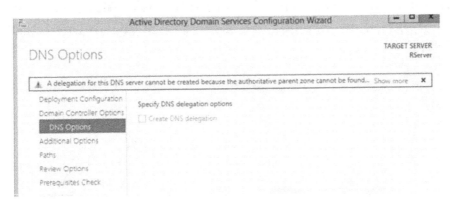

12) Because this is a new domain, there will be no existing domain servers to confirm the name. Continue with the installation.

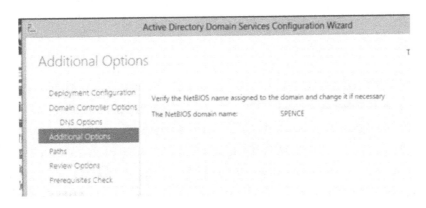

13) Some domains have other systems such as "Windows Internet Naming Service (WINS) which require a NetBIOS name. WE can accept the default and continue.

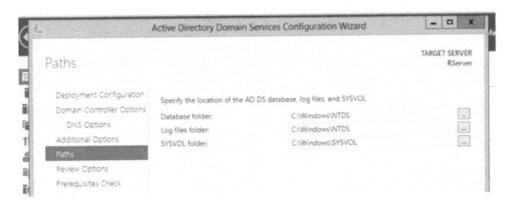

14) The three directories take up large amounts of space and in addition require multiple services which could slow the processes (Especially "Shutdown" and "Restarts". Best practice is to place each area on a different partition. For our exercise, we will accept the default and continue.

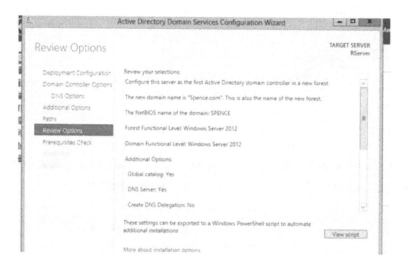

15) A finalized list of requested settings will be displayed for review. After reading, click "Next" and "Install". After a few minutes, the server will automatically restart and display the name of your domain. Click the "Administrator" icon and when server manager loads, you will see new items in the dashboard such as "AD DC" and "DNS". You have successfully installed a domain controller. Congratulations!!!

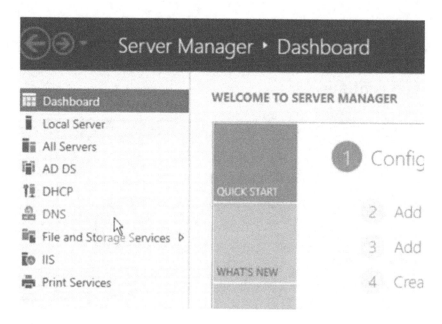

FSMO Roles and Migration:

When installing Windows Server as a "Domain Controller", it is essential to be to understand that there are other software "services" which are active on the single server. In truth...there are actually 5 different server services running on the server. At any time...if any one of the server services cease to function, then the results can be cataclysmic for a network. We refer to these services as "Flexible single master operator". Each service is responsible for a different aspect of active directory. The following are the functions and roles of each FSMO:

- **Schema Master FSMO Role** = In charge of changes and updates to the naming context of the active directory schema (Some people call this the "Naming Context" for the domain. There is only one schema master per directory. There can only be one in an active directory forest.

- **Domain Naming Master FSMO Role** = In charge of the entire forest name space of for the creation or removal of domains and sub-domains. This server might also control references to domains external to the domain of the domain controller. There can only be one in an active directory forest.

- **RID Master FSMO Role** = In charge of the creating and tracking Security Identifiers and Relative Identifiers within a domain. This FSMO can either add, remove or transfer SID's and RID's to other domains during migrations. This role can exist on many servers as in one server in each domain within an active directory forest.

- **PDC Emulator FSMO Role** = This master operating keeps the time synchronized between clients within the domain. The purpose of the time service is to ensure that the Windows Time service uses a hierarchical relationship that controls authority and does not permit loops to ensure appropriate common time usage. There are other aspects of an active directory which this server supports such as password changes, account lockout settings and also interaction with legacy server platforms such as Server Windows NT, Server 2000 and Server 2004. This role can exist on many servers as in one server in each domain within an active directory forest.

- **Infrastructure FSMO Role** = This FSMO keeps track of SID's associated with specific objects (i.e., Users, Printers, Shares, etc.) in reference to the objects distinguished name across different related domains. This role can exist on many servers as in one server in each domain within an active directory forest.

- **Important Non-FSMO Role in Active Directory:**
  - Global Catalog Servers allow searches in any domain in within the active directory forest. Think of this Server as a "Master Map" of everything in specific domain. There is a searchable copy of the location of every object related in any way to the domain. Every domain controller can essentially be a Global Catalogue server with the benefit that user logins will be faster. The only caution is that the global catalogue role should not exist on the Infrastructure FSMO due to conflicts with updating objects.

The importance of the FSMO's cannot be stressed enough. By default…the first server installed into the domain as a domain controller will contain all of the roles. In normal operation, if the network is extremely large,…the single server can be over-burdened. In addition, if the server were to ever fail,…the entire network would cease to operate. It is always in the best interested to have the ability to move the FSMO roles in the case of a server upgrade or in response to a failing server or possible malfunction.

There are a number of ways to perform migrations such as using a GUI interface within different snap-ins as well as a CLI method. Many network administrators prefer the CLI method because it can be easily accessed using the CLI on any computer in the domain that has access to a Microsoft utility called "NTDSUTIL". In addition, there are two methods which can be used to move the roles from one server to another as in the following:

- **Transfer** = This is the normal preferred method. Using this method,…the server which is destined for the roles requests approval from the existing FSMO role holder and the role is moved after the original server approves and updates active-directory that the move will occur. This method normally occurs during maintenance, upgrades or replacement of Domain Controllers.

- **Seize** = In this method,..the destination server begins performing the FSMO roles and advertises itself as the new FSMO role holder. This method is normally used when the original FSMO role holder is unresponsive or totally off-line. Once a FSMO role is "Seized", the original domain controller should remain off-line and never placed back into active service on the network. Below is the process for migrating FSMO roles from one server to another.

1) **Access the command line of a system and perform the commands to locate the present locations of the FSMO's:**

```
C:\>hostname
SERV2

C:\>netdom query fsmo
Schema master              SERV1.Cool.com
Domain naming master       SERV1.Cool.com
PDC                        SERV1.Cool.com
RID pool manager           SERV1.Cool.com
Infrastructure master      SERV1.Cool.com
The command completed successfully.
```

2) **We want to move the roles to "SERV2". Start the process by using NTDUTIL to connect to the destination server:**

```
C:\>ntdsutil
ntdsutil: roles
fsmo maintenance: connections
```

```
server connections: connect to server serv2
Binding to serv2 ...
Connected to serv2 using credentials of locally logged on user.
server connections:
```

3) **You can now "Quit" to move the prompt back to "fsmo maintenance" and move a role. We will select the "Schema Master" role:**

```
server connections: quit
fsmo maintenance: transfer schema master
```

4) **A confirmation dialogue box will appear and the move will process the move after clicking on "Yes":**

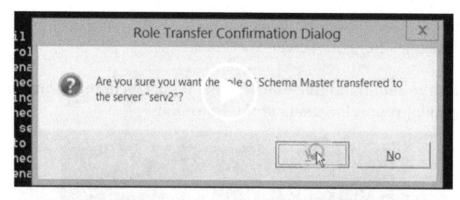

5) **We can now quit out of NTDUTIL's and observed how the moved FSMO role displays:**

```
C:\>netdom query fsmo
Schema master              SERU2.Cool.com
Domain naming master       SERU1.Cool.com
PDC                        SERU1.Cool.com
RID pool manager           SERU1.Cool.com
Infrastructure master      SERU1.Cool.com
The command completed successfully.
```

Notice now that the Schema Master now resides on Serv2.

Each role can be moved using the same process from up above. In the event the original server is off-line and there is the need to forcefully transfer a role the same commands are used except the word "transfer" is replaced with "seize" in the command.

Configure DHCP Services on Member Server (Non-Domain):

*Notes: You must be logged in as "Administrator" to perform the actions required for this task. Be aware that this exercise can temporarily disable a network if the server the lesson is being performed on is connected to an existing network which has a functioning DHCP server. It is HIGHLY RECOMMENDED that the servers used in this exercise be DISCONNECTED FROM THE FUNCTIONING

PRODUCTION NETWORK and connected to a small lab environment using an isolated switch or hub.

The following is an example of using installing "Dynamic Host Configuration Services" on a Server 2012 member server. The listed steps are not all-inclusive. More detailed instructions are displayed in the videos associated with this exercise.

1) **Activate Server Manager and select "Add Roles and Features":**

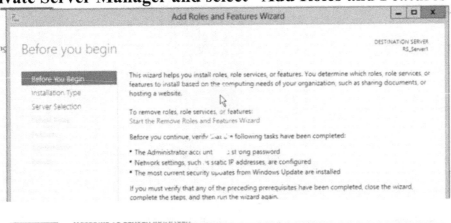

2) **Assure that your server name appears and the correct IP address exists:**

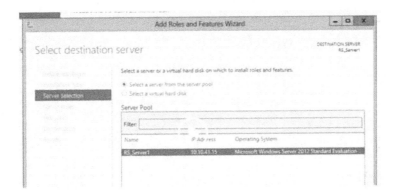

3) **Select the features for "DHCP" Server,..if any recommendations for additional required features appear, accept them and continue:**

r roles

Select one or more roles to install on the selected server.

Roles

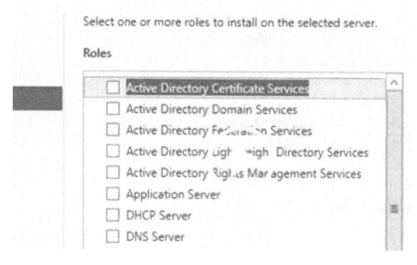

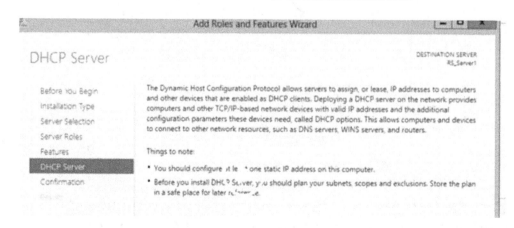

4) **At least two different confirmation scripts will appear allowing you to confirm your selections. Click "Next" on both.**

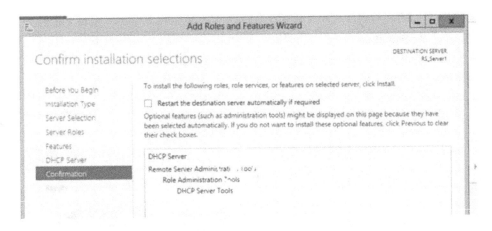

5) **After accepting script reviews,..the installation will begin. This process only installs the DHCP services. After the installation, you must configure the server for all settings it will distribute to clients.**

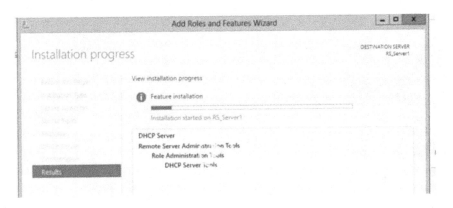

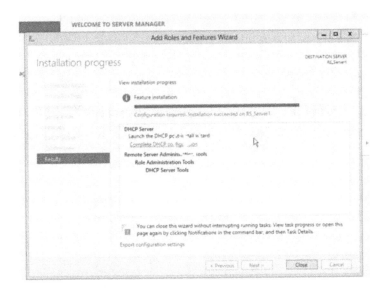

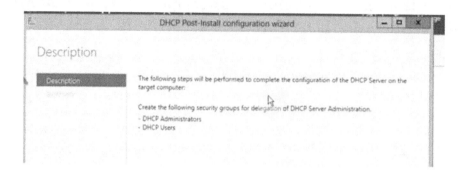

6) Click "Finish" and access the DHCP Snap-in from the dialogue box that appears of on the Server Manager "Tools" menu.

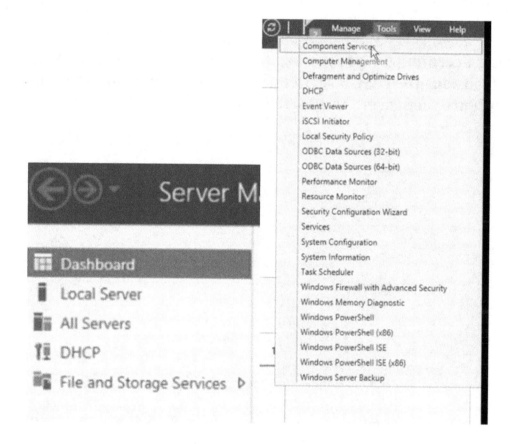

7) Expand the "DHCP" MMC to review controls for IPv4 and IPv6. Expand the extension for IPv4 to begin the process for creating a new DHCP Scope.

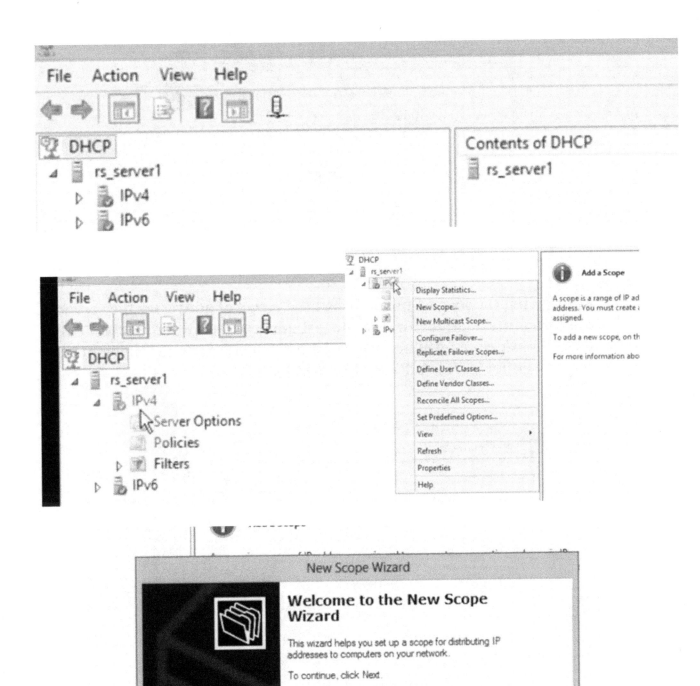

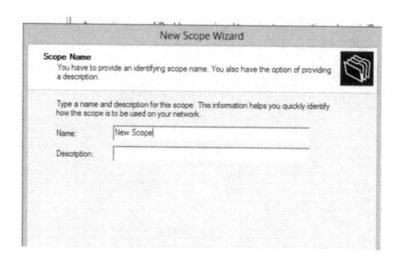

8) **After giving the scope a name, insert the range of addresses the server will distribute from the first to the last address. In addition, include the subnet mask which will be associated with the IP address (Note: You may use either "Classfull" or "Classless").**

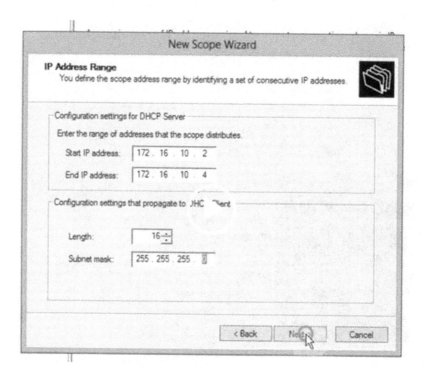

9) **If there are any addresses within the range you DO NOT want the server to distribute, place them in the list of "Exclusions".**

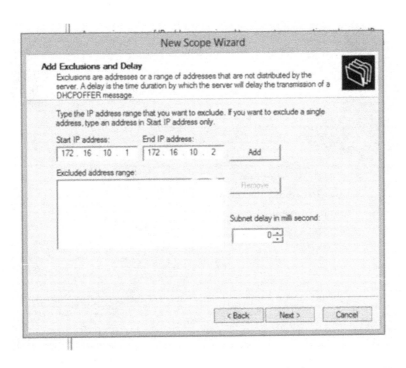

10) You may customize the duration a client is allowed to retain an IP address before it must make another request to the server.

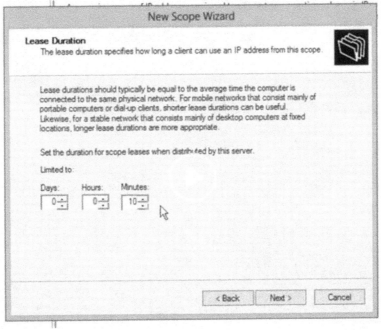

11) The prior settings were primarily for network communications INSIDE of a network (Or "LAN"). The remaining settings are concerning allowing the LAN clients to communicate outside of the network, such as to connect to the Internet. If your network will connect to the outside world click "Yes, I want to configure these options now".

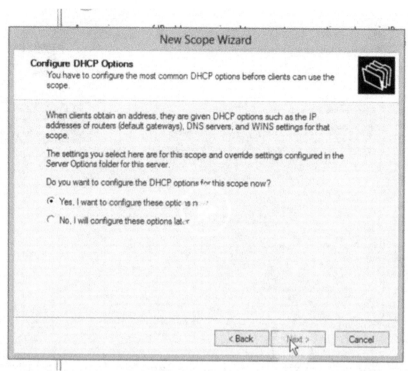

12) The "Default Gateway" allows clients to access networks outside of the specific network they are within.

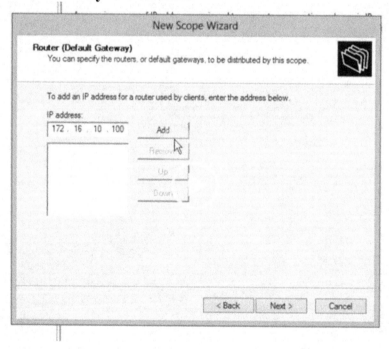

13) This setting allows the user of "FQDN" and "Domain Names" to locate resources inside and outside of the network. Click "Continue" and the system will pause for a minute or two to establish settings.

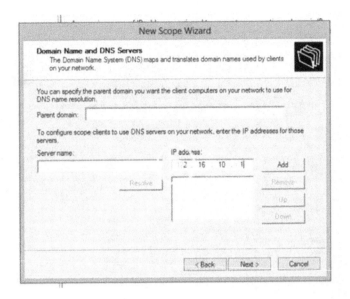

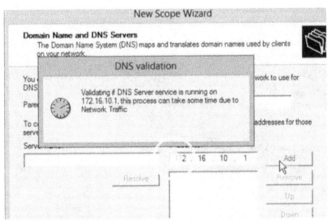

14) **Windows Internet Naming Services (WINS) may be active on the network. This setting allows clients to also know how to connect to resources which use NetBIOS names on the network. Click "Next" to continue, followed by "Yes, I want to activate the scope now".**

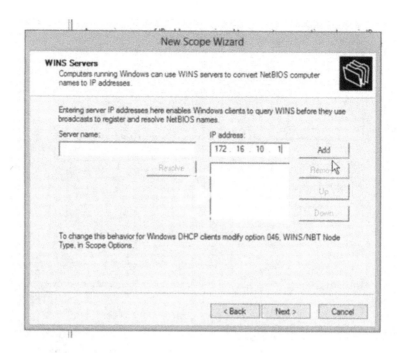

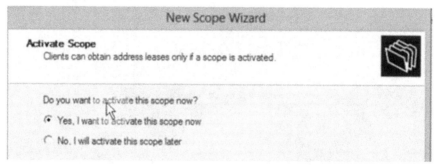

15) **After a few moments, the DHCP MMC will populate and the new DHCP scope will appear.**

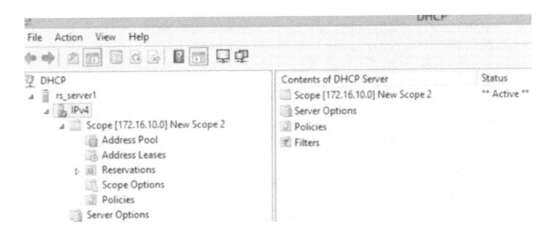

Creating Local Users on Server 2012 (Non-Domain):

*Notes: You must be logged in as "Administrator" to perform the actions required for this task. The following is an example of using a method of creating users which exist only on a specific 2012 Server. These users will not exist or have any other control of any other computer whether it is a server or a Windows 7 or Windows 10 client. The listed steps are not all-inclusive. More detailed instructions are displayed in the videos associated with this exercise.

1) Access the "Computer Management" MMC using either "Search" or "Windows Tiles".

2) Expand the "Local Users and Groups" Snap-in and "Right-Click" the "Users" extension. This will review a menu for creating "New Users".

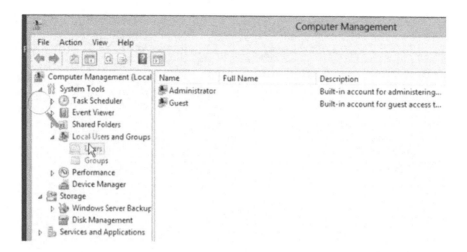

3) **After adding each new user, click "Create". The new users will not appear until after you have clicked the "Close" button. You may add as many users as you desire and continue using the "Create" button. All will appear after you click "Close".**

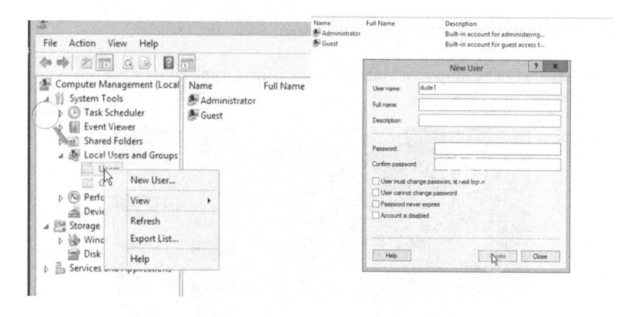

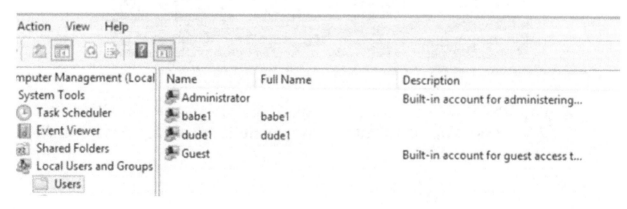

Creating Domain Users Server 2012 (Requires Domain Controller):

*Notes: You must be logged in as "Administrator" to perform the actions required for this task. The following is an example of using Active Directory Users and Computers (ADUC). The listed steps are not all-inclusive. More detailed instructions are displayed in the videos associated with this exercise.

1) **Using the "Search" option or "Windows Tiles", locate the "Active Directory Users and Computers" MMC.**

2) **Select the "Users" extension and it will display all default categories of users and groups which presently exist in active directory. It is possible to add new users here. It is best practice, however to create a "holding unit" called a "Container" to separate created users from default users. In addition, you can also create new groups, printers, folders and many other objects using this extension. The following pictures are very self-explanatory so there will not be written instructions for this process.**

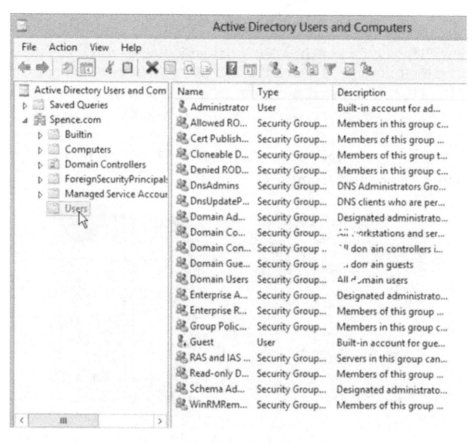

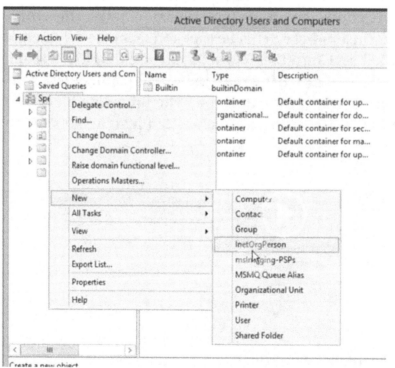

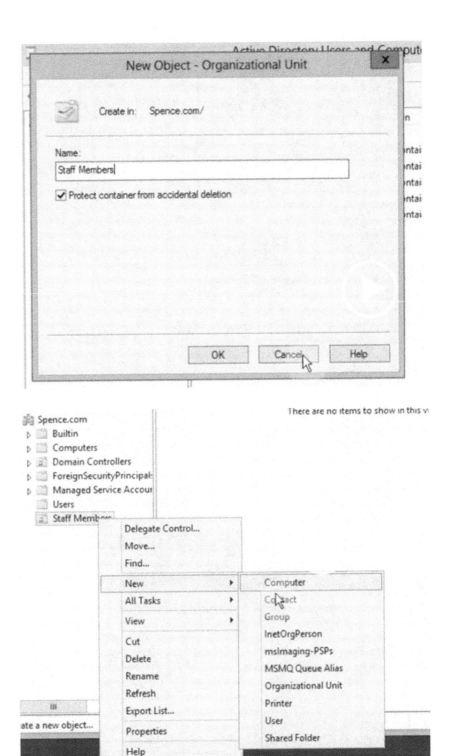

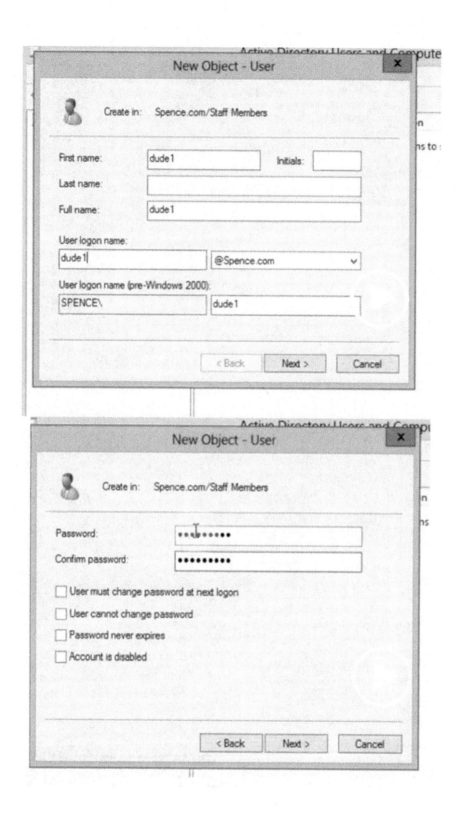

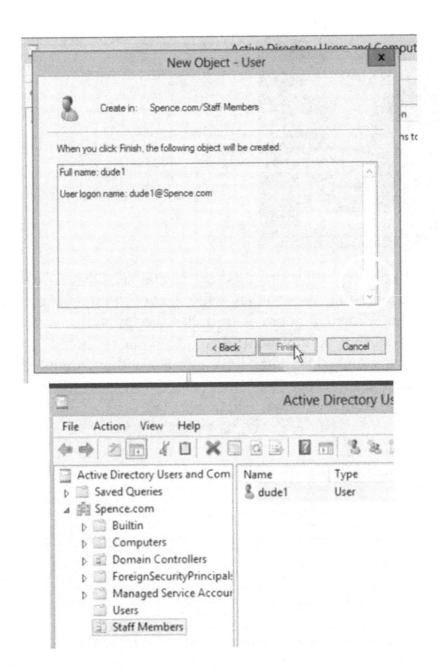

Creating Home Folders:

The following is the process for creating home folders for users. This folder is accessible for the user from anyplace on the network and can also be accessed over the internet outside of the company. This project assumes that you already have a domain controller, a client and users created. In addition, a folder called "Home" must be properly shared out on the Domain Controller. Using the Client, we will log in as a user named "Joe".

Checking "File Explorer" notice that this user has no "H:" drive. We will configure the account of the user so they will receive a home folder to be classified as "H: drive". The following picture is from the Server. Notice that we have a folder in "C:" drive of the domain controller shared out as "home". We will now modify the user's account so they will have a folder within "home" which will reflect the user's name.

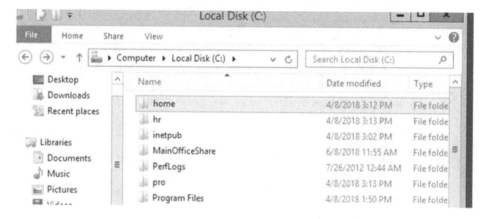

The following steps are required to create a home folder and attach it for that user. We must use "Active Directory Users and Computers" and locate the account we desire.

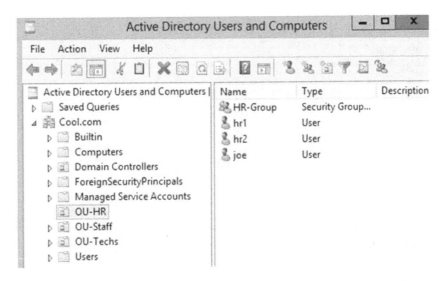

1) After locating the users account, we access the "Properties" of the user and then access the "Profile" tab and the "Home Folder" path. Here we insert the path for the user's home folder:

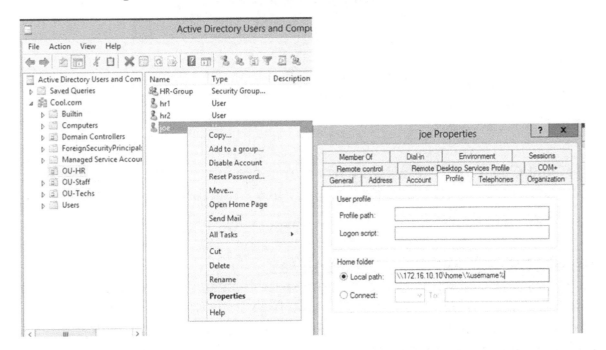

2) Here we selected the drive letter "H:". This will appear on whatever computer the user logs into. Notice that we inserted "%username%" in the path. This command will automatically create a folder for the user. After clicking the "Apply" button, "%username%" will update to the actual user's name. Upon inspection of the "Home" folder on the server will display a directory with the user's name.

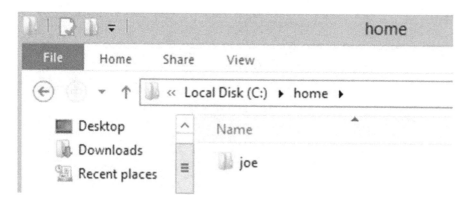

3) **Let us go to the client, login as the user and check "File Explorer" to see if the home folder appears.**

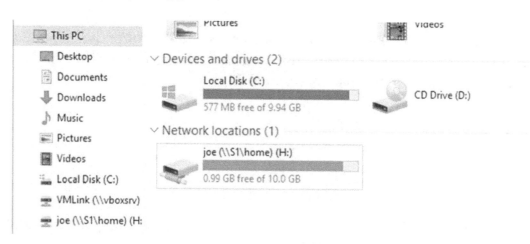

4) **And Cha-Pow!!! The home drive appears for that user. Anytime the user stores anything in this folder,...they can access the data from anywhere on the network.**

File Resource Manager – User Quotas:

Oftentimes, users continue to use up more space than a company or organization approves. On older networks, if there was a file server which had a total of 200GB of available space,..it was possible for a single user to monopolize the space limiting the use of the remainder for other accounts. Through the use of some management snap-ins on Windows Server,...it is possible to limit the amount of space which is utilized by particular users or groups. This process is performed with the use of "User Quotas" within the snap-in entitled File Resource Manager.

"User quotas" is a setting which limits the total amount of space utilized by individual users on a specific directory store. This type of setting is normally applied to a directory on the network which many users have access in order to swiftly exchange files with one another. The process is initiated utilizing the following elements:

- Shared Directory (These steps are outlined in the "Example Lab Configurations" chapter under "Creating a File Share").
- File Resource Manager installed on network.

1) **After the creation of the shared directory, activate File Resource manager and activate the "Users Quota" sub-snap-in:**

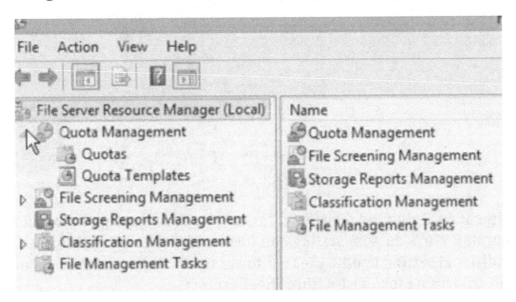

2) **There are a number of methods for creating the rules for the user quota. One way to start is to browse for the directory on which the quota will be applied:**

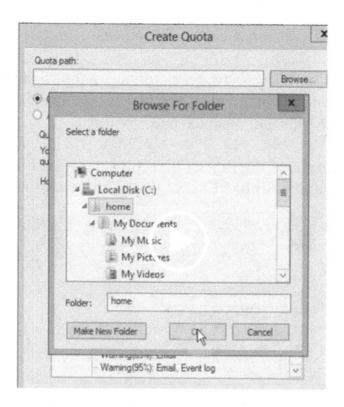

3) After identifying the directory, then the type of quota is selected from templates or a custom setting can be established. In addition, an additional setting can be created to create the individual quota on any sub-folders which exist within the directory.

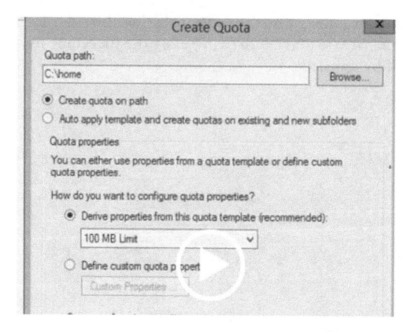

4) All the quotas are complete. Now if a user attempts to add files in excess of the amount specified in the quota, the users will be prohibited

or receive a warning that they have exceeded their allotted amount of space. The warning will look similar to the graphic below:

File Resource Manager - File Screening:

"File Screening" is a setting which limits types of files saved by individual users on in specific directory store. This type of setting is normally applied to a directory on the network which many users have access in order to swiftly exchange files with one another. The process is initiated utilizing the following elements:

- Shared Directory (These steps are outlined in the "Example Lab Configurations" chapter under "Creating a File Share").
- File Resource Manager installed on network.

1) **After the creation of the shared directory, activate File Resource manager and activate the "File Screening Management" sub-snap-in:**

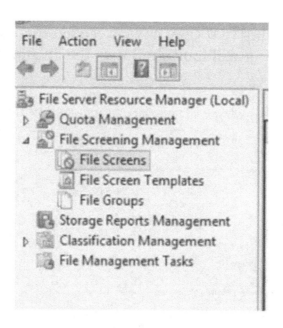

2) After selecting "File Screening Management, continue to "Create File Screen" which will allow you to browse to the directory of which is being configured and to identify the types of file that are prohibited:

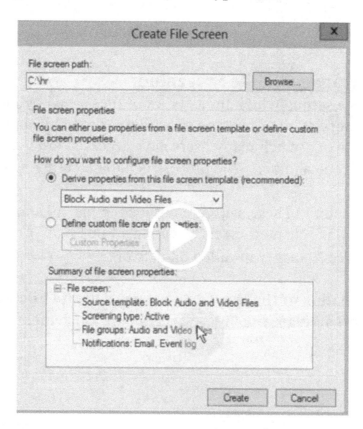

3) With file screens, you can select different types of files. The above example are music and video files. We will move the screen to

concentrate on programs which can be installed or run on the computer. These types of files are called "Executables" or simply "EXE's":

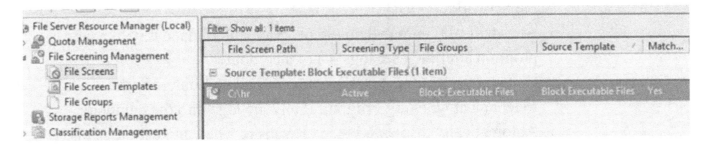

4) The settings for the file screen are now complete. Any user which attempts to store an executable file will be stopped. The notice the user will receive will look similar to the following graphic:

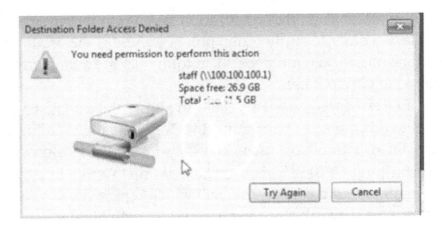

Group Policies Overview:

Group Policies are an aspect of Windows Server Active Directory. Group policies attempt to provide a service which simplifies the maintenance, support and management of a network utilizing Windows and clients. The following are the elements of Group Policies:

- **Identify a service, process or object** = This could be access to a specific directory, a program or printers.
- **Identify a person or group** = Examples might be the "CEO of a company", the "Executive Team", or "Summer Temporary Employees".
- **Method of access** = How the service, process or object will interact or be available to the person or group.

- **Examples Group Policies used in a company or business:**
  - Allow all persons in the "human resources" to receive access to a shared directory entitled "Employee Manuals" from any computer in the network.
  - Automatically uninstall an old program and replace it with a newer program after the user logs off of a computer.
  - Connect the "AutoCAD 3D printer" to all computers in the Mechanical Drawing Program if anyone logs into the computer.
  - Automatically display a video or website when any user logs into a company computer.
  - Perform maintenance tasks on computers after the system is started (Bootup).

Group policies can affect an entire organization, a subgroup of an organization or an individual user. In order to apply group policies, there is the requirement to implement various objects and methods. The following are some terms for the elements required in Group Policies:

- **Group Policy Manager** = This Snap-in allows the establishment of policies to be enforced in an active directory domain. Within the Group Policy Manager, you have many sub snap-ins and extensions.
- **Organizational Units** = This is created within "Active Directory Users and Computers" to create an "object" which represents logical collections of items in the network. The items could be individual users, individual computers, groups of either, printers and many other objects.
- **Scripts** = These are fields which perform tasks which are associated with the policies. Examples of scripts are often "VBS" files and even older legacy files called "Batch" files.

Using Group Policies, a network administrator can control access to a large array of resources without ever leaving their desk or work area. Group policies may also be used on "stand alone" computers, although this is rarely done unless there are a very few computers which must be managed. When Group Policies are only on a stand-alone computer, they are referred to as "Local Group Policies". When Group Policies exist on a Domain they are called "Domain Group Policies". There is the option of having both "Local" and "Domain" group policies, but by default, "Local" policies will overrule "Domain" policies unless the Domain policies are set to "Enforced". The following are some utilizations of Group Policies.

Group Policies for Printers:

Printers are a device which traditionally get the most use on networks. Depending on the work environment, printers can be local (Directly connected to a computer) or network-based (Accessed via a wireless network connection or some other manner in which the printer is not directly connected or controlled by the user computer). Printers are often replaced, upgraded or installed for specific users. Printer Group Policies are an ideal method for enhancing the access for printers as well as the control needed for network administrators in their everyday support of printers on a network.

Printer group policies have a number of functions such as printer software installation, upgrade or removal per user, group computer. One feature often used is to deploy access to printers via group logins. Printer deployment is one of the areas of group polices which is illustrated in this textbook.

In the following passages, we will illustrate the process of implementing Group Polices. We will also utilize other objects which support Group Policies such as "Groups" and "Organizational Units". In order for this project to be completed, it is necessary to have the following installed on an active directory network:

- **Server Print Management.**
- **Group Policy Manager.**
- **Active Directory Domain Controller.**
- **Installed printers to be deployed.**

1) **We begin by checking Active Directory for our users and groups. You can see we have associations for "Staff" and "Human Resources (HR). We presently have some test users in both groups.**

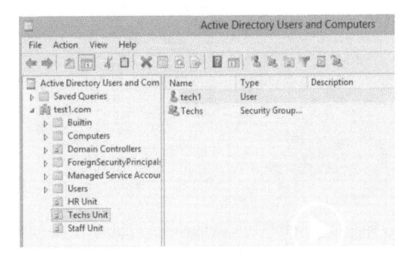

2) **Note: Notice some OU's have an "icon" on them. These are OU's to which group policies can be applied. OU's without are "Default OU's" used by the system and will not accept group polices. We can close out that snap-in and go to "Devices and Printers". You see we have a few printers installed with similar names to the groups and OU's.**

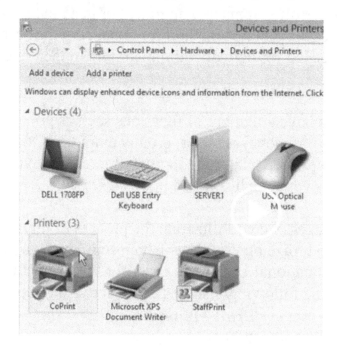

3) **We need to connect the printers to the groups. In order to accomplish this task,..we will combine two additional snap-ins called "Group Policy Management" and "Print Manager". Let us access "Group Policy Manager".**

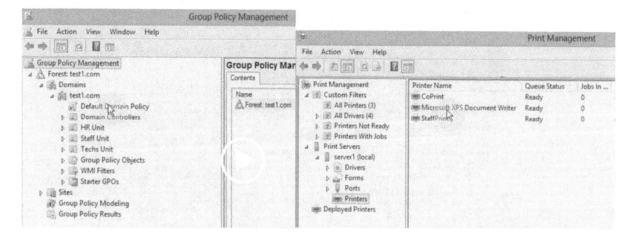

The Group Policy snap-in controls rules which are applied to groups within the OU's. The rules are separated by domains. In this domain, we have OU's for

Staff, HR and Technicians. Let's create a rule for all the people that are part of "staff". In this rule, we desire those that are in the Staff group to always receive access to a network share and a printer. In order to create this Group Policy rule, we must assure the existence of the following elements:

- Installed Printer (These steps are outlined in the "Example Lab Configurations" chapter under "Adding a printer to a Server").
- Shared Directory (These steps are outlined in the "Example Lab Configurations" chapter under "Creating a File Share").
- Script to connect the users in the group "staff" to the shared directory. This could be a simple script called a "batch file" which is created by saving a notepad document with the extension of ".bat" as opposed to ".txt". We would have to user a network mapping command followed by a "UNC (Universal Naming Convention)" such as in the following picture:

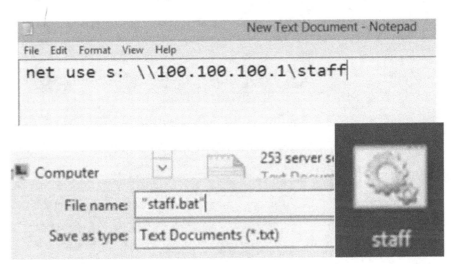

Now we create a policy on the domain which we can associated with the printers, shared directories. Some of the steps are below. First we "right-click" the domain in Group Policy Management and select "Create a GPO in this domain and Link it here.." (Note: By default…policies are created for all users on a domain as soon as they are attached. We only want this rule to affect "Staff" so we will modify the policy soon after. Conversely, we could create the policies in the "Safe Area" called "Group Policy Objects" so they are not active):

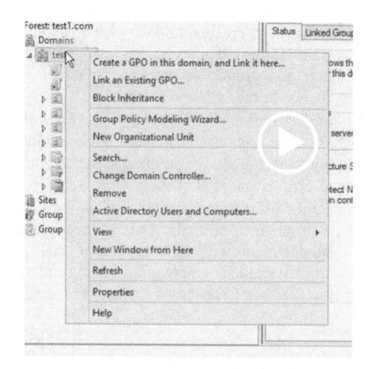

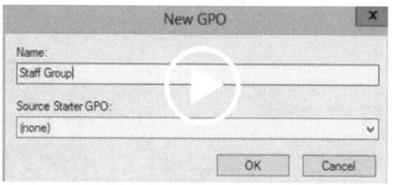

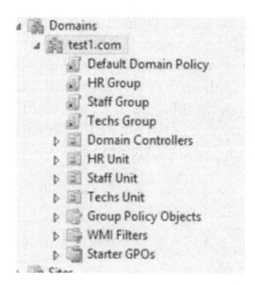

We created a policy for "Staff". Remember, however that when we create a GPO, it automatically affects all domain users. Let's modify the GPO for HR and see how we must take out the default for "Authenticated Users" and replace it with the particular group we want the policy to affect which will be the "HR" users. We would start by "double-clicking" the HR Group GPO and then click "OK" when the warning box appears.

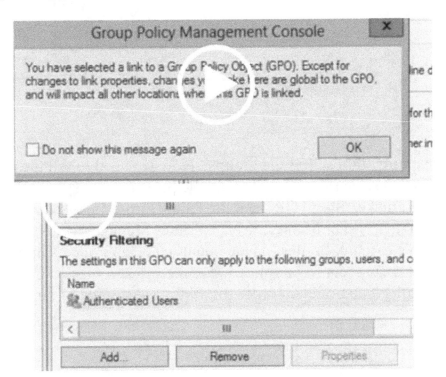

You now would simple remove the "Authenticated Group" and replace it with "HR Group".

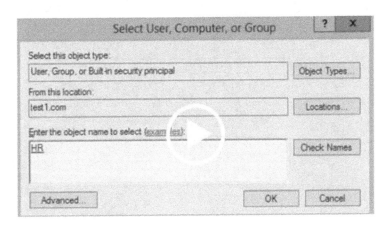

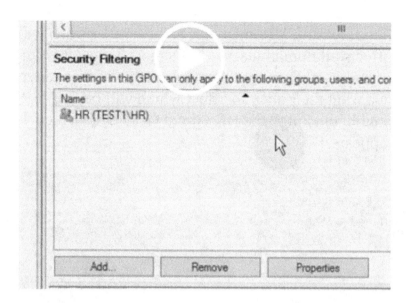

There is now a policy for each of the groups. Now we need to tell the policy what it should do. In this scenario,..we will make the policies give specific users printers. We will make "Staff" GPO get the "Staff Printer" To accomplish this,..we must go to "Printer Management". Printer Management controls printers for a domain. We can link Printer Management to Group Policies in order to give the printers to specific users. The following is the process for deploying the Staff printer to the Staff group policy in order for all the users in the group to get the printer:

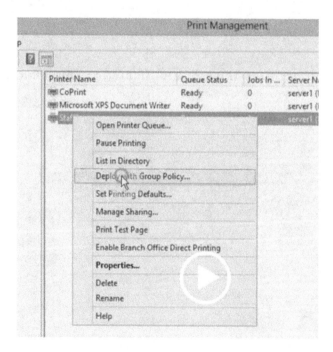

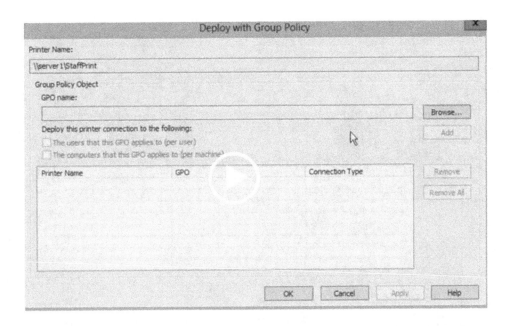

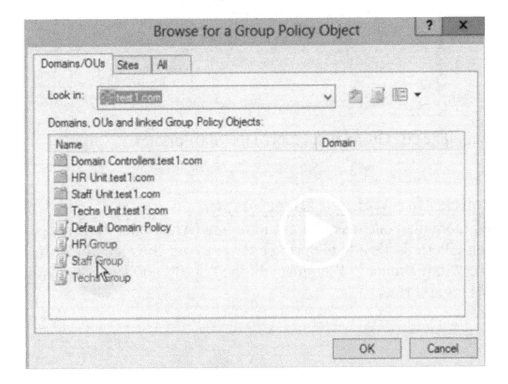

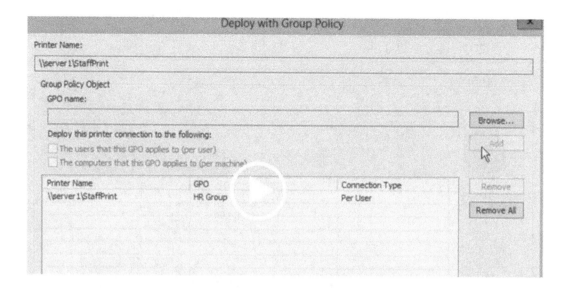

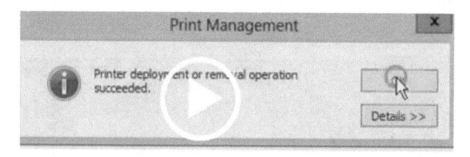

Now all users for Staff Group will receive the Staff printer.

Group Policies for Mapped Directories:

We can add more than one task to a group policy (Although best practice is one rule for each GPO). Let's add the printer script to the GPO so all "Staff" users get access to the "Staff Printer". We must edit the "Staff GPO" and locate the area which holds login scripts:

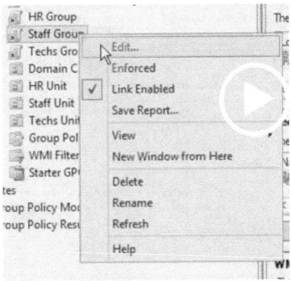

1) **Once the GPO opens, you must navigate to the "Logon" section:**

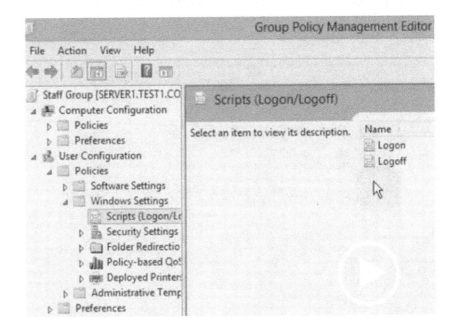

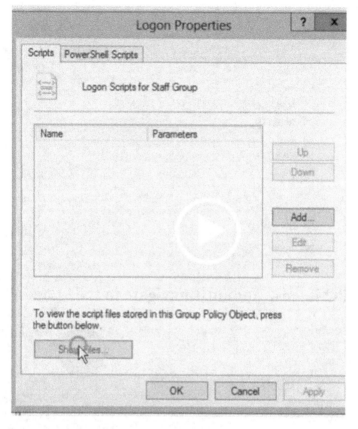

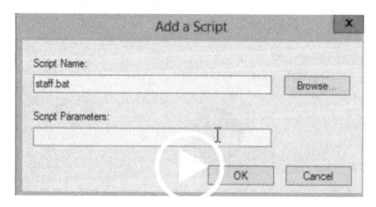

Now when a user from the "Staff" group logs in, the will receive both the network share and the printer for their group.

Roaming Profiles:

Roaming Profiles is the ability for a user to retain their "customizations" for their desktop GUI. Icons on their desktop, options in their Start Menu, their screen "Theme" and even the photo on their desktop can display on any computer on the network.

The following is the process for allowing desktop settings to move across computers when a user accesses different systems. This project assumes that you have already installed a domain controller with the proper roles. In addition, you will need at least two clients and a domain user to test the profile.

On this installation, we have created a user named "Joe". We have also created a folder called "pro" to hold all the user profile data. Let us configure the user's profile settings. To start, we will locate the users account and then access the "Profile" setting under the "Profiles" tab:

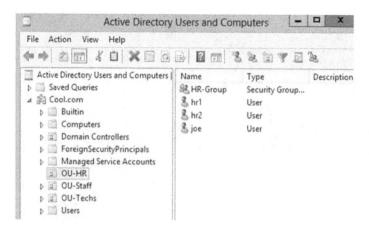

Here we selected place the path to the profile folder in the "Profile" field. Notice that we inserted "%username%" in the path. This command will automatically create a folder for the user. After clicking the "Apply" button, "%username%" will update to the actual user's name.

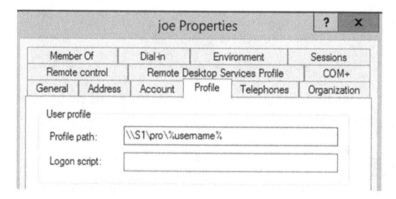

The process is complete although no folder will appear for the user until they successfully login and then logout. All of the user's settings, documents and themes will now follow the user regardless of whatever client the user's accesses.

Creating a Shared Resource using the CLI:

Sharing a resource on windows systems can be performed using either a GUI or CLI. Obviously, using a GUI is far simple for standard computer users. When using a GUI, it is required to create or locate the resource, activate the resources' "property sheet" and configure "sharename", "permissions" and "security" settings. The following is an abbreviated example of using the CLI to create a share.

1. **CD** = This is a helping command to move you to the root of whichever drive you are using.
2. **Mkdir <Desired name of directory>** = This creates a directory.

3. **Net share <Desired Name of Share>**=<DriveLocation and name of directory to share> = This makes the directory accessible from the network.
4. **Net share** = This command without following parameters displays any shared directories or resources on your system.

The following is an example of creating a share and assuring its existence using a CLI:

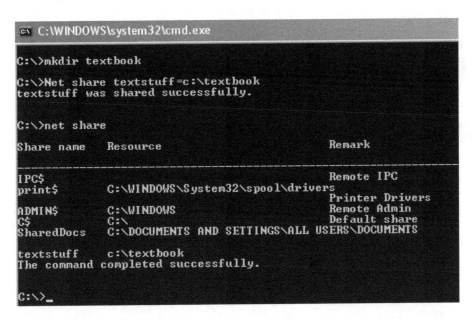

To eliminate the share via command line, perform the following:
1. **Cd** = As stated before, moving to the root of the drive.
2. **net share <sharename> /delete** = This command removes the share function.
3. **Rmdir <directory name>** = This command will delete the directory.

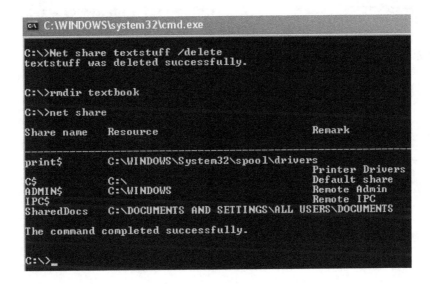

Removing Security Settings on a Windows Client or Server:

With this example, we will totally disable all security to make access easier. When you work on a computer in an office environment, the settings will be more customized. The following list is not all-inclusive and the associated videos are more detailed.

1) **Make sure all firewalls are off.**

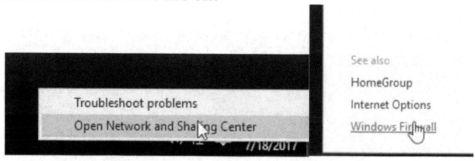

2) Make all the "Green" icons turn "Red".

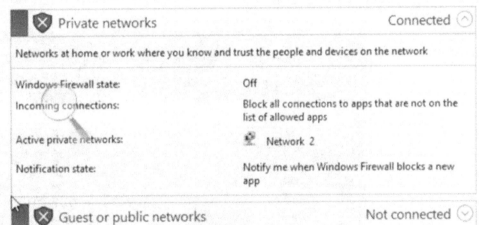

3) Turn off "Password Protection".

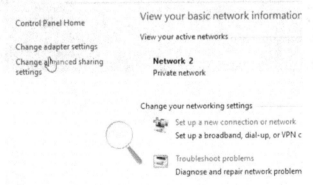

Typically, Windows manages the connections to other homegroup computers. But if you have the same user accounts and passwords on all of your computers, you can have HomeGroup use your account instead.

- ⦿ Allow Windows to manage homegroup connections (recommended)
- ○ Use user accounts and passwords to connect to other computers

Guest or Public ⌄

All Networks

Save changes | Cancel

Password protected sharing

When password protected sharing is on, only people who have a user account and password on this computer can access shared files, printers attached to this computer, and the Public folders. To give other people access, you must turn off password protected sharing.

- ⦿ Turn on password protected sharing
- ○ Turn off password protected sharing

Save changes | Cancel

4) Assure you have the correct IP address and other computers can ping the IP address.

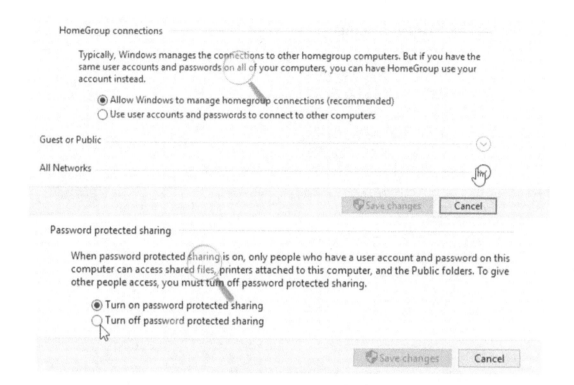

5) Create needed folders inside of "C" drive (Some of these folders are used for other exercise).

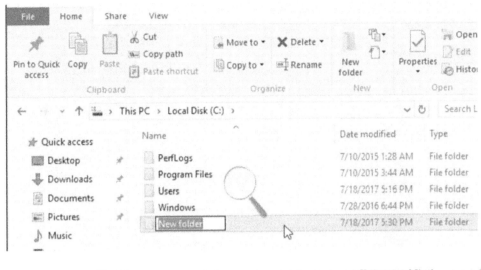

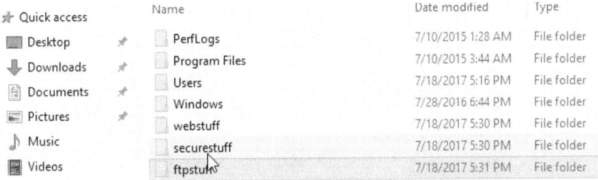

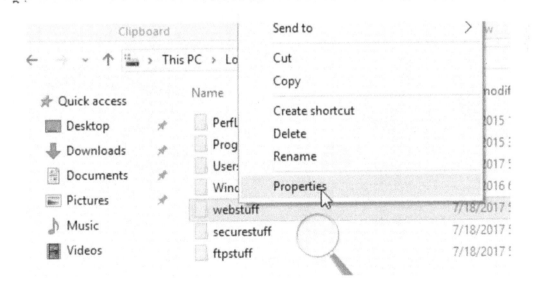

6) Configure "Share" permissions on each folder.

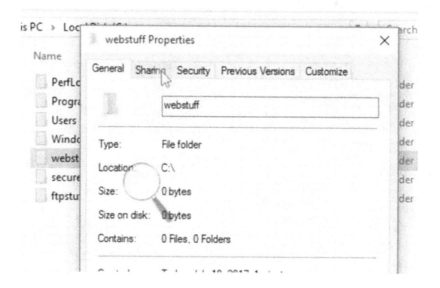

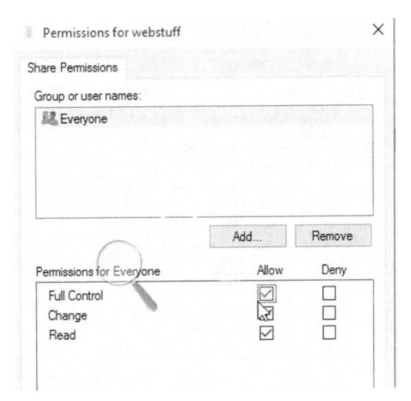

7) Configure "Security" permissions on each folder.

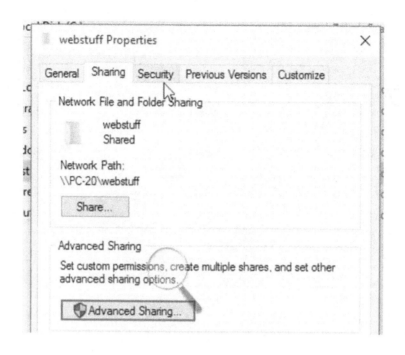

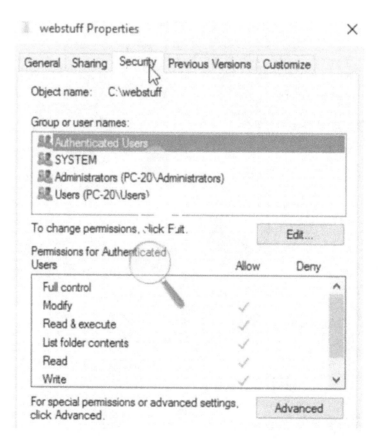

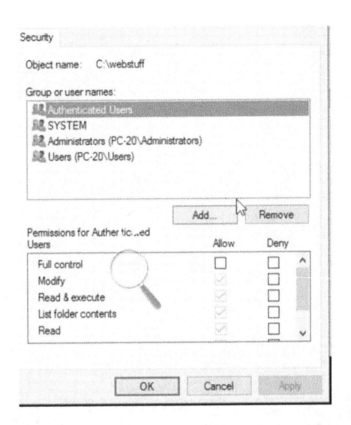

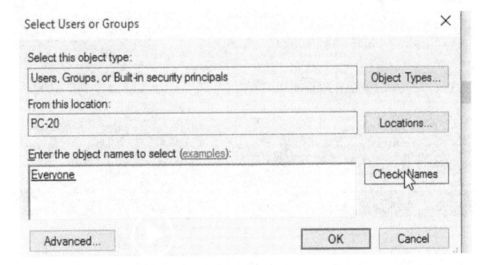

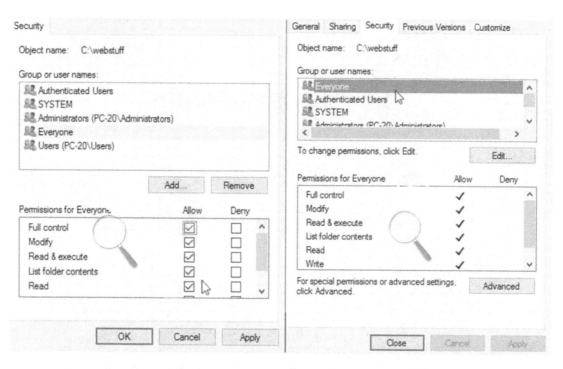

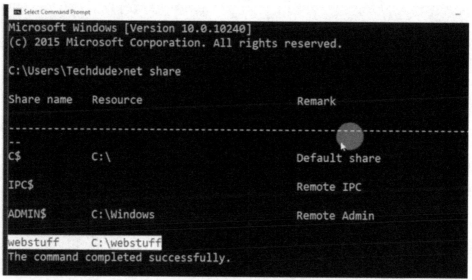

8) **Check to assure that the folders are shared two ways:**
  ➢ **"Net Share" utility:**

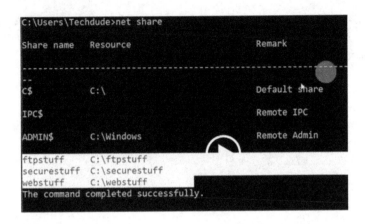

  ➢ **"UNC" method:**

9) **Now anyone on the network who can "ping" your computer will be able to access any files you place in the shared folders.**

Naming (Renaming) a 2012 Server (Non-Domain Controller):

*Notes: You must be logged in as "Administrator" to perform the actions required for this task. The following is an example of using a method of naming or renaming a Window 2012 Server. The listed steps are not all-inclusive. More detailed instructions are displayed in the videos associated with this exercise.

1) **Access Server Manager and click on "Local Server" under the "Dashboard" window.**

2) **The name of the server will be displayed in "blue" to the right of "Computer Name". The default name for most Window Server installations begin with "WIN-###########". Double-Click this area to display the properties dialogue box for the server's name and membership.**

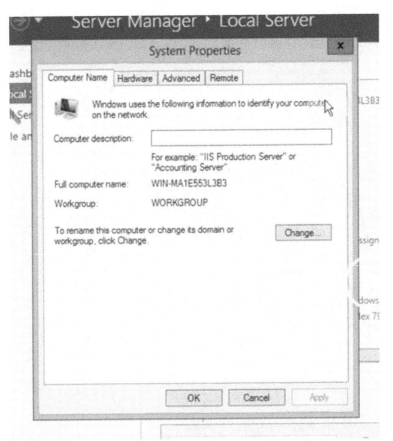

3) There now appears a new dialogue box displaying a field to give the computer a description along with the server name and what group to which the server belongs. Click the button on the middle-right which states "Change…".

4) **It is here in which you place the new name of the server. Type in the new name and click "OK". Afterwards, the computer will inform you that it requires a restart to establish the change. Click "OK" and the subsequent "Restart". After the server reboots, user either a CLI or a GUI to assure the name has been changed.**

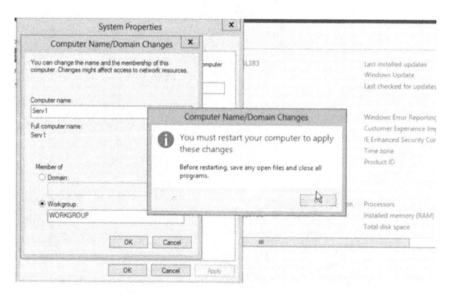

Adding a Windows 10 Client to an Active Directory Domain:

*Notes: You must be logged in as "Administrator" to perform the actions required for this task. The following is an example of using a method to add a Windows 10 client to an Active Directory Domain. The same process is used to add many versions of Windows to domains (i.e., Windows 98, 2000, Vista, Win7 and Win8). The listed steps are not all-inclusive. More detailed instructions are displayed in the videos associated with this exercise.

1) **Prior to adding the client to the domain, we must establish an IP address on the client and assure that it can communicate with the domain controller for the domain we will be joining. Utilizing "Networks and Sharing Center", we will access the computers network interface.**

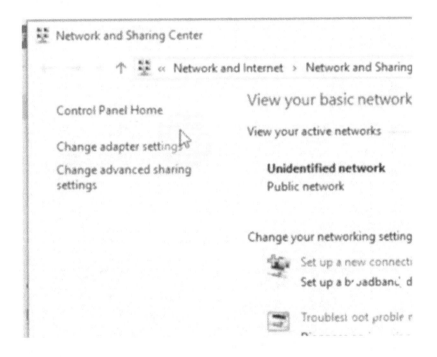

2) **Double-Click "Change Adapter Settings" (Called "Ethernet" in the illustration) and then right click the Network Adaptors properties.**

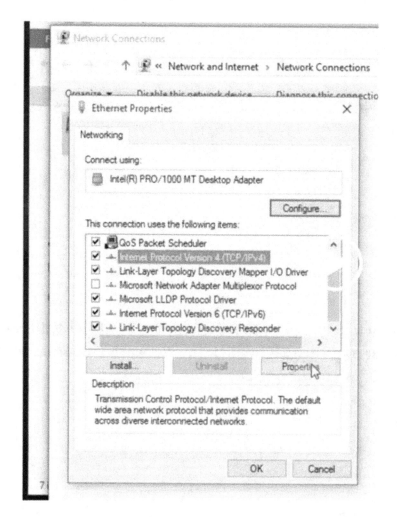

3) Select "Internet Protocol Version 4" (DO NOT UNCHECK THE BOX) and then select "Properties" in the lower right corner. The dialogue box which appears requires at least placing an IP address, subnet mask and Preferred DNS settings. The other areas may be skipped for this exercise.

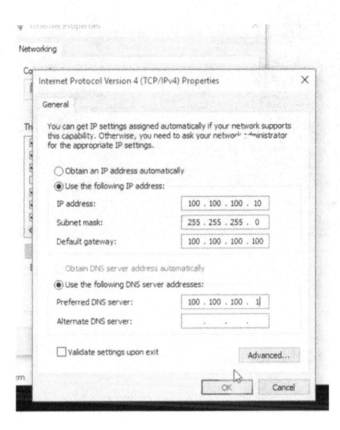

4) After placing the IP configurations, click all "OK" and "Close" buttons and open a CLI. From the CLI, attempt to ping the IP address of the Domain Controller (Which is "100.100.100.1" in this exercise).

5) **After successful ping replies. Access "This PC" and "Right-Click" to bring up the PC properties.**

6) **The bottom-third of the display will show the present "Computer Name". Double-Click the "Change Settings" button to the right of the computer name. This will display the name properties to allow changing the computers description and other sub-features.**

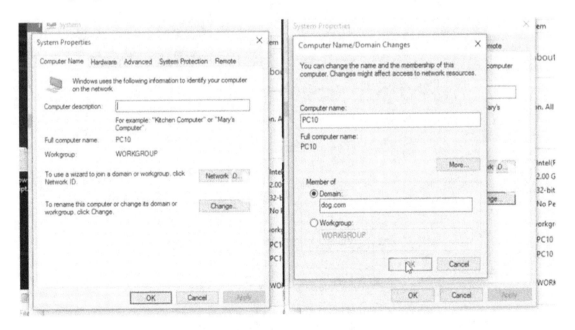

7) **From this area, you select "Change" towards the bottom-right of the dialogue box which will display a dialogue box to change the name or make the computer a member of a domain. Place a "dot"(.) in the radial button (That means the "Circle") in front of the word "Domain".**

Follow that action by typing in the name of the domain you want the computer to be part of.

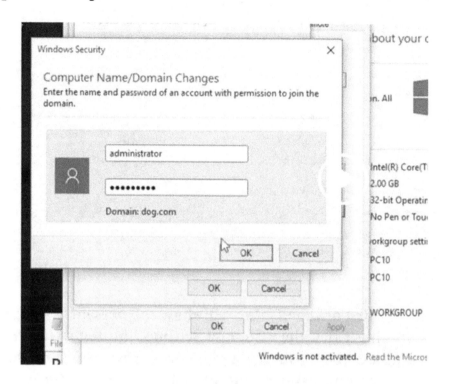

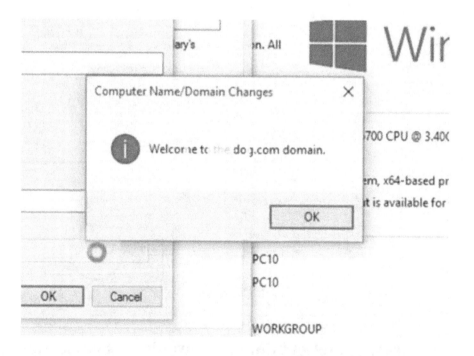

8) **A security dialogue box will appear requesting the username and password of an administrator for the domain you are attempting to join. Insert the credentials and click "OK". If you use a non-domain**

administrator account, the attempt will be rejected. If you have used a valid domain administrator account, you will receive a "Welcome to the Domain" message and be required to click "OK" and "Restart" about two times each to establish the domain connection.

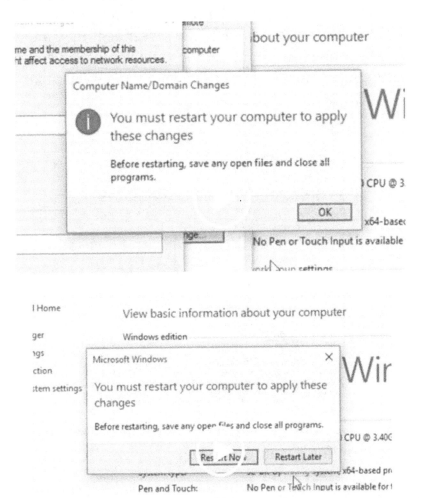

9) After restarting the computer, access the computers Properties" sheet again and you should see a display of the computer's domain membership.

Enabling Remote Desktop:

"Remote Desktop" is used to allow a client or server to be accessed over a network (Or the Internet) from a remote location. This is often done so a technician is in one city and is required to service a server in a totally different city, state or country. As long as the server or client has electricity and an active network connection, approved users can manipulate the server as if they are directly in front of the computer. The following are the settings which must be configured. First, access the "Property Sheet" for the server for which you would like to control as in the following:

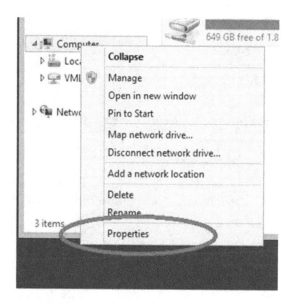

1) **On the properties of the server, access "Remote Settings" to continue the configuration for Remote Desktop:**

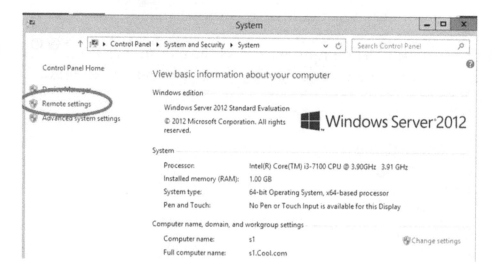

Within the System Properties for Remote desktop, there are a number of the following options such as:

- Different levels of security.
- Configuring "Remote Desktop Rights" for users (By default, the "Administrator" has the "Remote Desktop Users" right.

2) In this lab, we will keep the simple settings by placing a "dot" in the "Allow remote connections to this computer" button and uncheck "Allow connections only from computers running Remote Desktop with Network Level Authentication (Recommended)". We only do this for "practice". On corporate settings, we would not remove this setting.

3) Now the server will connect remote connections. There are a number of methods available for connections. We will utilize Microsoft "Remote Desktop Connection" method. Using a Window 10 client, we can locate "Remote Desktop Connection" under "Windows Accessories":

In the "Computer" field,..the identifier of the computer you wish to control can be listed in the format of a FQDN, hostname or IP Address. After clicking "Connect", the client will attempt to contact the server. After successfully contacting the server, Windows Security dialogue box will appear requiring a "Remote User" with the appropriate credentials. After account validation, the server will issue a security certificate to protect the communications which must be accepted (This will sometimes not appear when logging in as an "Administrator"). Following the certificate acceptation, the desktop will display the identity of the server with a "Tab" at the top of the screen and the desktop of the server will be displayed.

From this point, the server can be totally controlled via the Remote Desktop Connection.

Conclusion of the book:

You have reached the end of this text and I hope it has benefited you greatly. In the writing of this book, it was my desire to impart knowledge and methods which readers could use to increase their understanding of Server and Network technology. In addition, many sections are directly dedicated to both building network infrastructures as well as gaining technology-related certifications. I hope you have profited from my work and I wish you great success in all your adventures in network technology. Remember, ..."Knowledge First in All matters!!!!"

CPSIA information can be obtained
at www.ICGtesting.com
Printed in the USA
LVHW061813040819
626455LV00015B/440/P